Stop Teaching

Lyle,

Thank you for your
mentorship and
friendship.

Isabel
Sep 2016.

Stop Teaching

Principles and Practices for Responsible Management Education

Isabel Rimanoczy, EdD

Stop Teaching: Principles and Practices for Responsible Management Education

First published in 2016 by
Business Expert Press, LLC
222 East 46th Street, New York, NY 10017
www.businessexpertpress.com

ISBN-13: 978-1-63157-379-8 (paperback)
ISBN-13: 978-1-63157-380-4 (e-book)

Business Expert Press Principles for Responsible Management Education Collection

Collection ISSN: 2331-0014 (print)
Collection ISSN: 2331-0022 (electronic)

Cover and interior design by Exeter Premedia Services Private Ltd., Chennai, India

First edition: 2016

10 9 8 7 6 5 4 3 2 1

Printed in the United States of America.

Abstract

What do we need to change in order to develop a new generation of business leaders who connect profits with purpose, who see in social entrepreneurship and innovation the key opportunity for addressing our planetary challenges? The answer lays in the contents we select to teach, in the values we invite to explore and develop, and in the methods we use.

In the era of 24/7 global access to information from our mobile gadgets, many institutions of higher education are still sitting students in rows or amphitheaters, measuring success via tests and evaluations, with instructors lecturing what students should learn. And instructors feel the challenge of competing with sleepy audiences that divide their attention between their cell phones and the speaker.

Stop teaching, the author says, inviting instructors in management schools and higher education to adopt some proven learning principles that can reengage students, unleash their potentials, and foster them to shape the world they want to live in. And have fun doing it.

Through adult learning research, guides, activities, and stories from pioneering learning facilitators in education and corporate training, Rimanoczy brings a long-needed revamp to educational institutions that want to be part of responsible management education.

Keywords

action learning, action reflection learning, adult learning, andragogy, blended learning, empowering students, holistic pedagogy, student engagement, teaching adults, teaching for sustainability, UN PRME learning methods

Contents

Foreword

On the Eve of Management Education's Finest Hour

By David L. Cooperrider

Nearly 12 years ago I joined with Nobel Laureate Kofi Annan, then Secretary General of the United Nations, and hundreds of CEOs from corporations such as Green Mountain Coffee Roasters, Daiwa Asset Management Ltd, Siemens AG, IBM, Tata Industries, Novo Nordisk, China Mobile, Royal Dutch Shell, Dow, Coca-Cola, Starbucks, Novartis, and others such as the microenterprise pioneer Grameen Bank. Unexpectedly, at this Leaders Summit in the UN's General Assembly Hall, we learned that we shared a common conviction: *that business has the opportunity to be one of the most positive and creative forces on the planet, and that the epic transition to a world economy of "full spectrum flourishing" is no longer a utopian urge or minitrend, but an observable and remarkable trajectory.*

That day over 2,000 stories of sustainable value (good for the world and a pathway to superior business results) poured in: business as a force for eradicating extreme poverty; business as a force for ecoinnovation and human flourishing; and business as a catalytic agent for peace in some of the most extreme conflict zones in the world. The stories of innovation and leadership were inspiring and successful: factories and buildings being designed in ways that serves to give back more clean energy to the world than they use; bottom-of-the-pyramid strategies and microenterprise models demonstrating how business can eradicate poverty through profitability; circular economy organizations designing products that leave behind no waste—only food; and macrowikinomics—everything from telepresence to megacommunity—all showing how we may be rebooting our capacity for human cooperation and global action. It was a remarkable summit and I was totally privileged to have been selected to facilitate the event using our powerful large group planning and codesign method of Appreciative Inquiry.

For me there was one major disturbance, however. It was a total surprise. And to truly understand it you have to remember who was in the summit. It was almost all *CEOs*—not their representatives. The good news was how these top leaders in business—I was at a table with CEOs from the likes of Novartis, Royal Dutch Shell, Tata, BP, Unilever, and Dow—all of them embraced sustainability not as a "bolt on" or old-fashioned social responsibility or philanthropic appendage to the business, but as a "core" to business strategy, the creation of stakeholder value, and preparing for long-term business horizons. Lord Brown from BP was at my table, for example, and he just this year published a Harvard Business Review article declaring that the appendage view of CSR "is dead." It was the same with all of these CEOs at the table—every one of them thinking 50 to 100 years out; all thinking about the industry leading innovation potential of the lens of embedded sustainability; and all sensing the total eclipse of "the great tradeoff illusion" or the belief that doing good can only be an additional cost to the business; and all seeing how the search for mutually beneficial advances between industry and the world's most pressing global issues has become one of the defining issues of the 21st century—I then asked them a question. I asked them a question about scaling up this kind of excellence: "What's the toughest challenge you face in scaling up your sustainable value successes?" Their answer was something like this:

> The biggest challenge is dealing with our mid-managers who because of their past training still see these things as sidelines to the business, and it is also hiring young managers out of business schools who have no idea of the priority essence of sustainable value thinking as the core to strategy.

In other words, what the CEOs were saying was that there is a top to bottom gap. While *their* jobs required them to think in sustainable value terms *strategically*—thinking in terms of shareholder value *and* stakeholder value including human value, ecological value, and community value simultaneously—the schools doing the management education of their people were way behind. One CEO whose company was now defining sustainability not as simply doing "less bad" but as leaving a net-positive fingerprint, turned to me and asked bluntly: "How many of your faculty at the business school are really out here in the real world; do they ever sit down with CEOs like me because they just don't seem to get it—sustainability and things such as socially responsible leadership cannot be a sideline in our business or a public relations activity—why are business school students still coming out debating if social responsibility is good or bad for a business?"

I could go on a rant articulating how far behind our management schools are, that is, how far behind they are from today's C-suite realities and why, but the better question is this: "If anything imaginable were possible and we could re-invent management education for 21st century realities and beyond, how might we design learning environments to inspire the next generation of globally responsible leaders in ways that create not laggards but the 'the firms of endearment' and industry-leading stars of tomorrow?"

This book by Isabel Rimanoczy is one I've been secretly waiting for a long time, perhaps ever since that 2004 eye-opening UN Global Compact Leaders Summit, where the CEOs I candidly deliberated with were so far beyond what we are still teaching in our management schools. And guess what? I also think this is the book that every one of those leaders will love. They, every single CEO I met and worked with there, passionately wants our schools to cultivate our next generation managers to aim higher. They desperately need management education, responsible management education, to succeed. "There can be few people in business today that could doubt," said Patrick Cescau the group CEO of Unilever, "that social and environmental sustainability will be *the* defining business driver for multinational corporations in the first part of this century."

This is a book that unites the best in learning theory with the worldwide movement to educate globally responsible managers who possess the mindsets and mental models, the positive leadership qualities, and the intrinsic sense of purpose needed to *unite* success with significance, doing good with doing well, and the design-thinking skills needed to help turn every single social and global issue of our day into a business opportunity. Most of all it's a treasure trove for teachers, a wonderful resource guide for anyone wanting to return to the deepest roots of the term education, that is *educare*, which in Latin means "to lead forth" and "to bring out from within." John Dewey once reminded us just how privileged a position it is to be an educator when he said: "Education is not preparation for life, Education is life itself."

For people who have been around Isabel Rimanoczy, they know how she elevates everyone around her and brings all of this to life with her students. She is a masterful educator, seeing the best in each human being, and she inspires more than instructs, cultivates more than convinces, and does orchestration more than oration. I've seen her students—alive and creative, passionate and purposeful, and inspired and self-directed in their learning—and it's a joy to experience. The reason I raise this here is that there is an authenticity to Isabel's life as a teacher that's in total congruence with what she has written here: *this material is not just the stuff of abstraction, but is as real as it is powerful.*

But please beware as you read on. Her title provokes us with the mantra "Stop Teaching" and this, to be sure, is no empty phrase. It's a serious and radical invitation to rethink almost everything we do as educators. While we each know deep down, for example, that experiential learning creates learning environments that engage all of the senses, we still find ourselves as "the sage on the stage" more than designers of experiences. And we forget the towering lessons of Albert North Whitehead, in his classic, *The Aims of Education.* Do you remember Whitehead's three most important components of cultivating "knowledge alive" instead of "inert knowledge"? There are three phases: (1) the phase of *romance*; (2) the phase of *precision*; and (3) the phase of *fruition*, that is bringing our knowledge to full flower in the real world. But the phase that is the #1 most important—and the one that gets buried and bypassed in most business school settings—is the phase of romance, that is, the lighting up of such love for the learning where it is like a romance, head over heels, where the passion is so high that no stone will stand in the way of discovery. In management education, how many of our classroom's magnify and excel in this, the great phase of romance?

This book is a gift. For me—while reading—it became something of a positive dislodgement of certainty. It reminded me of what really matters and it brought me face-to-face with the fact that in all of the inertia and pressures, I too often turn away from the courageous creativity needed to touch the soul of another person, to design anew everyday, and to put deep learning into the operating system of management education.

While I was studying this book I found myself imagining many things: What might our management schools look like if they were designed in ways that looked more like an IDEO or Apple design studio—alive with collaborative teams; alive with rapid prototyping; alive with possibility thinking with real clients in the room—how might that change the phase of romance? What might the classroom look like if reflective practices— mindfulness meditation; journaling; and listening for "what is the call of our time?" or "what's the future that is wanting to happen?"—were indeed deeply woven into every section dealing with living values in business? And what might my classroom look like if I took seriously the concept of intergenerational mentoring where I could help link students with the most courageous and successful, flourishing and sustainable enterprise pioneers on the planet, perhaps an Elon Musk or Judy Wicks, and have them do biographies of "business as an agent of world benefit"—much like John F. Kennedy did with his "Profiles in Courage."

In this I need to give a shout-out to Isabel Rimanoczy's generative leadership role in a management educator's dream website supported by the United Nations Principles for Responsible Management Education (UN PRME) initiative and Case Western Reserve University called www.aim2flourish.com that does just that. It's a worldwide appreciative inquiry into "business as an agent of world benefit"—a search for what's best, what's next, and what's possible—where professors can directly link their management students with entrepreneurs and executives creating the new story of business for good. I've seen it up close on many occasions now: how it transforms lives, inspires new careers, and lifts people's sights. It unites the original promise of the Internet with experiential learning, while creating relationships that reverberate. And it's so simple, and free, to bring into the classroom.

For me Isabel Rimanoczy's message is threefold. The first is that it's an incredible time to be alive in the field of management education. Second, it's about reminding us what a tremendous privilege it is to be in this field touching so many young leaders' lives. And third, it's about revitalizing our courage to teach for *responsible* leadership because, as Isabel so aptly puts it: "such an education is not about data, but about making meaning, about empowerment and action."

Read this book reflectively. Let it help you rethink education in more holistic ways—mind, body, heart, and soul—and let it help you to design the classroom of your dreams. For this is something we never should stop doing—that is, reinventing our teaching. And lucky for us: here is the perfect reminder!

David L. Cooperrider
Fairmount-Santrol Professor of Appreciative Inquiry
Weatherhead School of Management, Case Western Reserve
University and Champlain College's David L. Cooperrider Center for
Appreciative Inquiry
April 22, 2016

Acknowledgments

It is always a magical moment, when I sit down to reflect who are the individuals I am indebted to for the role they played in you reading this page, today. Pioneers like Lennart Rohlin, the MiL Institute's "crew," together with Ernie Turner and the LIM founders, who ventured into a different way of experimenting with learning. The power of Action Reflection Learning (ARL) intrigued me to research and attempt to code the methodology, and over decades I continue finding new ways and settings to apply the principles, and honoring your pioneering work. Victoria Marsick, Lyle Yorks, and Jeanne Bitterman, from Teachers College at Columbia University, you mentored me through my discovery of what helps adults learn. Boris Drizin and Paul Roberts were the intellectual teammates who helped distill the theoretical foundations and define the principles: my gratitude goes to you. Thank you Jonas Haertle, who said to me, "Yes, do it!," when I mentioned my idea to write about the learning principles that I had been using to transform the traditional way of teaching Oliver Laasch who said, "I support you," and the colleagues of Business Expert Press. To Tony Pearson, whose patience is continuously challenged by my creative "Spanglish" expressions, and who has been my editor for 20 years now, helping me learn and elegantly shaping my writings. To Anders Aspling, for his thoughtful comments and suggestions to make this a better work. And to my inner circle of friends, at LEAP, the UN PRME Working Group on the Sustainability Mindset, at Nova Southeastern University, at Aim2Flourish, Mariam Tamborenea, Clara Arrocain, Veronica Legrand, Silvia Leon, Sandra Sowelu, my dear family and friends who are my "fan club" that shows unconditional support and encouragement, to all of you my endless gratitude. To Martine Marie, the Universe brought us together to do some very special things. My gratitude to you, for your playful and professional way of helping me imagine new horizons, and then following up in the details, all the while reminding me to go with the flow. To Martha Driemer, author in her 80s and my mom, for her feedback, inspiration, and presence as a role model for my life. To my dad, for the lightness of being he taught me. And to my dream and life partner, Ernie Turner: my gratitude for your continuous "why not?" attitude, that invites me to aim higher, and your "dream-plan-act," which became the mantra guiding my days.

I said it is a magical moment, because once we are aware of how we are all interconnected, the list of individuals who—knowingly or not—influenced this book becomes infinite. Their names go across geographies, and across time. So let me end with a humble acknowledgment: Accept my gratitude, and since I will never be able to pay you back, I will pay it forward and do my part, do my best.

Endorsements

How do we develop the enormous potential of young people who want to make a positive difference in society? It won't be enough to use pedagogical approaches from the past. We can and should reinvent learning, to more fully engage the passion and the creativity of the young, and connect learning to action. That's what this book is about. And it is why this book matters, for we cannot afford to underinvest in the talent that will make the world a better place.

Dan LeClair, Executive VP and COO, AACSB

Isabel's book provides valuable insights into how teaching, learning, and development need to be rethought for engaging learners in the 21st century. It is itself a compelling story line.

Lyle Yorks, Professor of Adult and Continuing Education, Teachers College,
Columbia University

Whilst many wait for the world to magically auto-integrate values of sustainability, Rimanoczy embraces her pioneer status and provides examples where innovative learning experiences have been designed and crazy ideas have been attempted. Right here is a book of kindness that could save us from falling into repetitive issues. We must take it as a call to action and start transforming the definition of learning itself. *Stop Teaching* calls on "teachers" and students to understand that the sustainability mindset is simply about focusing on the knowing, doing, and, most importantly, the being. Amongst others, inclusive, participatory and inspiring methodologies should replace the corruptive, divisive, and individualistic technique of solely grading.

"The show," certainly, "needs to be run together." We must realize that to attain a world where true leaders drive and strive, we have to treat education as a journey to fully be engulfed in, with mind and body, a journey of self-development, which we collectively create and own. It is time to embrace the "stop teaching" revolution and no one can be left behind because, as Rimanoczy well deducts, students are capable of owning their educational experiences, they just require a redefined "teacher" status—one that supports and mentors.

Anita Negri, President Oikos International, Geneva, Switzerland

In clear and accessible language, peppered with vivid vignettes of real-life teachers, Isabel Rimanoczy envisages what it looks like when educators and trainers put aside notions of teaching to focus on learning. This is a must-read for anyone interested in actively and holistically engaging learners.

Stephen Brookfield, John Ireland Endowed Chair,
University of St. Thomas, Minnesota

Isabel Rimanoczy offers a practical guide to educating future business leaders who want to make a difference. Her revolutionary approach helps management educators strengthen new capabilities in students who want jobs with greater purpose. Rather than top-down presenting of data and analysis, Rimanoczy suggests that educators become learning facilitators and engage students in grass-root activities that generate new levels of creativity and collaboration aimed at business and world benefit. Her book offers a valuable learning methodology to engage young people's passion for work that is not only financially rewarding but also personally and socially meaningful.

Chris Laszlo, PhD, Professor of Organizational Behavior,
Case Western Reserve University

Stop Teaching: A long awaited book on the inspiring new principles of management education. This book should be a "must read" for every business school faculty. The approach offered will immerse students in the sustainable mindset through management education. It is my high hope that our business school institutions would all support this new value-based, purposeful management education approach. And the time is now, since Mother Earth and our world civilization is at stake!

Amelia Indrajaya Januar, Faculty of IPMI International
Business School, Jakarta, Indonesia

Today, innovative teaching practices have become a hot button issue for teachers, learners, and policy-makers in a community. "StopTeaching" attempts to raise our awareness of how to deliver teaching to our Apps generation—maintain interaction and create a platform to engage learners—and how to create an on-going dialogue and reflect on ways to learn. Isabel's book is a call to teachers, students, and involved stakeholders that change is needed for self-awareness and interconnectedness, for curriculum redesign and, the most important of all, for developing sustainable skills with a positive mindset for sustainability.

I hope this book not only gives us food for thought, but also soul for re-engineering in the pathway of building a knowledgeable society.

Dr Shirley MC Yeung, Director, Centre for Corporate Sustainability and Innovations (CCSI) Hang Seng Management College, Hong Kong

This book is just as relevant to leaders in general as it is to educators. It is just as much a book about leadership as it is about learning. One of the most important roles of a leader is to facilitate learning.

Stop Teaching should be required reading for anyone in a leadership role, or anyone who wants to move from a power position to one of personal authority. Most leaders spend the majority of their time in meetings. The concepts and suggestions in Isabel's book would make a big difference in executive boardrooms as well as in more everyday work meetings.

Lennart Rohlin, Founder and CEO, MiLgårdarna AB, Sweden

This book was developed through the insights and multivariate experiences of the author's educational and global journey and the practical advice is offered in a captivating way. It is an impassioned guide for transforming the way management education and higher education needs to change to meet the needs of new students and accelerate the change we wish to see and provides a holistic view of systems thinking and planetary challenges. The resource material is carefully backed by data and insights from research, colleagues, business leaders, CEOs, and other educators and coaches. *Stop Teaching* serves to reenergize educators to not only make a difference in the lives and learning of future leaders, it tells us how to do so.

Jeanne E. Bitterman, EdD, Core Faculty of Adult and Organizational Learning Teachers College, Columbia University

Stop Teaching is a thoughtful, inspiring, and purposeful book in which the author seeks to raise issues and challenges to higher education in management education, and promotes change in teachers, students, and directors of business schools and universities.

Reading this book challenges us to move beyond our comfort zone and to ask: are we doing the right thing in our classrooms? Do we understand the local and global reality and prepare our students to be leaders? It reminds us that education needs to be "student centered"; they come to us not only to receive information but also to learn how to develop new ways of being, to know and to act, and this requires teachers to go beyond "teaching" to make way for new pedagogical approaches, materials, facilitation, and learning spaces. Our goal must be to encourage our students to take responsibility for their learning, self-reflect, discuss, think independently, and take risks.

Consuelo García de la Torre, PhD, Full Professor of Management and Marketing, EGADE Business School, Tecnologico de Monterrey, Mexico

Isabel Rimanoczy sums it up well with the title of this timely and important new book: *Stop Teaching!* In an interconnected world undergoing transformational social and environmental change, the old pedagogy of "lecture-test-rinse-repeat" is simply no longer up to the challenge. The age of the expert imparting wisdom to the masses is over. Tomorrow's education must catalyze, engage, and promote action. This book not only makes the persuasive case for "why" but also shows us "how."

Stuart L. Hart, Steven Grossman Endowed Chair in Sustainable Business, University of Vermont, and author of Capitalism at the Crossroads

"The most important thing when you breathe is not to inhale or exhale, but to move back and forth between the two. A responsible manager is someone who is able to breathe and move back and forth both in time and in space. Like any 'conventional manager,' that means being able to focus on the short-term view as well as few stakeholders (customers, management, or shareholders). A responsible manager, however, is someone who is also able to think about the long term and to think systemically by taking the whole ecosystem into account when making decisions. Business schools have been very successful at teaching the short term and restricted stakeholder vision, but ecological, social, and economic crises prove that we need to reinvent teaching and to instill a more holistic approach in our students. This book is here to help you to learn to inhale. It sheds light on a range of successful approaches that have been implemented in universities across the globe. It is a source of inspiration for all instructors prepared to step outside their comfort zone and into genuine student-centered learning."

Jean-Christophe Carteron, Director of Corporate Social Responsibility,
KEDGE Business School, Developer of the Sustainability Literacy Test

Isabel Rimanoczy's *Stop Teaching* presents an exceptional argument for reflexive pedagogy and more engaging classroom practices. As a potentially formative text for many educators, *Stop Teaching* helps its readership to step out from behind the podium and instead create active learning experiences for students, trainees, and employees. By proposing an active framework of knowing, being, and doing for learners, Rimanoczy encourages educators to shift their focus from reliance on expertise and the banking model of education to a simultaneous consideration of several learning preferences. A truly effective teacher embraces a well-rounded approach that includes not only disseminating information, but also articulating purpose, facilitating application, and discussing implications. No matter the subject area, Rimanoczy's approach in *Stop Teaching* is gracefully applicable to educators who can—and should—learn how to set the stage and then get out of the way, encouraging learners to take charge of their own learning.

Molly J. Scanlon, PhD, Assistant Professor, Department of Writing and
Communication, College of Arts, Humanities, and Social Sciences,
Nova Southeastern University

As a founder of Globally Responsible Leadership Initiative (GRLI) and having experienced Action Reflection Learning (ARL) at MiL Institute in Sweden many years ago, I read *Stop Teaching* with recognition and familiarity.

ARL is placed in the midst of a huge question—"How can we develop in the most effective way a generation of responsible managers, who are able to take our civilization to an evolutionary breakthrough to shape a world that is sustainable, or even better, in terms of John Ehrenfeld, that is flourishing for all?"

Isabel Rimanoczy's book places the ARL principles in a current context, and they definitely survive the test of being both relevant and appropriate—and much needed. The author's detailed observations of the short-comings of many of today's learning practices and arrangements, thoughts on future development and explicit examples of a variety of tools for facilitating genuine and responsible learning renders a rewarding read. The dialogue between the author and the four "learners" is intriguing and filled with connections, associations, reflections, and explanations.

The author is thankfully not alone in embracing these values and practices, but rather contributes to what a growing number of learning institutions are in the process of exploring and implementing. Thus, the book contributes to a development in motion—in need of further promotion, enhancement, and enlightenment; ultimately to support the shaping of a world where we all are able to develop to our full abilities and where we share responsibility for all of us, and the planet.

Professor Anders Aspling, Founding Secretary-General of the Globally Responsible Leadership Initiative (GRLI), Professor, School of Economics and Management, Tongji University, Shanghai, China

Stop Teaching not only challenges us to rethink business education in a world where expertise is accessible to anyone with a smart phone, but also provides instructors with a framework and pragmatic examples on how we can meet this challenge and develop responsible interconnected global leaders. This book gives new instructors and seasoned classroom veterans food for thought on how we conduct our classes and relate to our students. Anyone who cares about effective learning should read *Stop Teaching*. It will make you reflect on how you teach long after you read the final page.

Rita Shea-Van Fossen, PhD, Associate Professor of Management, H. Wayne Huizenga College of Business and Entrepreneurship, Nova Southeastern University

Introduction

Principle # 3

How does purpose connect with planet and with theories of learning? It was the spring of 2005, and I was sitting at my kitchen table, looking at some magazines that featured stories of retiring CEOs and leaders who were sharing how they planned to actively engage in philanthropic causes now that they had the time. I wondered, what about while they were in their CEO position, did they ever ponder, then, how their decisions were impacting people and communities around the globe? What would the world look like if every leader considered the impact of their daily decisions on people and on the planet?

A few months after this I began to draft my research project for my doctoral dissertation. I wanted to study business leaders who actually championed initiatives that made a positive impact on communities or environment. I wanted to understand how they thought, what motivated them to act in such a "business-as-unusual" way. My thought was that perhaps there were some clues in answers to these questions, which would help us intentionally develop a new generation of leaders—leaders responsible and conscious about their impact on the planet and all life on it—people and economies included.

Through the lens of adult learning, I began my search to find some of those exemplary leaders, to interview them and hear about their personal journey, and also to explore how they learned to think and act the way they did.

Imagine my excitement when in 2006 I found a conference titled "Business as agent of world benefit," organized by Case Western University, in Cleveland, Ohio, that was suggesting profits and care for our world could go hand in hand. After several corporate keynote speakers had haughtily showcased their organizations as agents of substantial benefit to the world, someone on stage wondered: If these people are exemplars of innovative leadership, how are we, business school educators, contributing to the problems we see? What values are we teaching? What should we begin to do differently? These questions triggered a working group that a year later came up with the document "Principles for Responsible Management Education." The document included a list of areas for business schools worldwide to pay attention to, issues that they needed to review as they were preparing the young for the world that was happening outside the classroom. The principles pointed at the values we were teaching, the purpose of business we were suggesting, the collaborations, dialogues, and research we were targeting—and the learning methods we were using. Surprisingly, in a context more focused on the "what" than on the "how," one unexpected principle had made it into the list of six:

Principle 3. *We will create educational frameworks, materials, processes, and environments that enable effective learning experiences for responsible leadership.*

I was intrigued by the inclusion of such a principle, and it was not until a few years later that I was able to fully understand the importance of it. After completing my doctoral research and identifying a group of what I considered essential elements that could be intentionally developed—what I termed "the sustainability mindset"—I was invited to design a program to develop such aspects for graduate students at Fairleigh Dickinson University, in New Jersey. Working on the learning outcomes, contents, and materials, I soon realized that the "how" of the program was as important—if not more—than the "what."

Responsible leadership calls for a combination of knowing, being, and doing, which cannot be simply taught. It may not even be possible to develop it fully, but we have multiple ways to inspire, foster, challenge, invite, motivate, intrigue, excite, engage, all of which can create a fast track to achieve those ambitious goals of preparing a new generation ready to shape the world we want to live in.

This is what this book will present.

The principles section has been written with the four learning styles in mind, addressing the "why, what, how, and so what questions" of the readers. Based on the work of Bernice McCarthy[1] and David Kolb,[2] the voices of these different learning preferences are brought into the book, because they are real and happen all the time. And while learners normally have a combination of preferences, there is frequently one that is stronger than the others. The book will apply a name to a "person" who will serve to demonstrate each of the four learning preferences. Julia represents the voice of the **Why learner** (someone interested in why we should care about the topic, what is the problem we are addressing); interested in the purpose and rationale; the **What learner** is Nick, interested mainly in theory and what experts have to say. A comfortable learning environment is in the classroom with an "expert teacher" lecturing or reading a text; the **How learner** is Andres, who is primarily interested in how we apply what are discussing, how we bring theory into the classroom; he is comfortable in a safe laboratory-type environment discovering the steps; and Vivien, who speaks for the **So What learner**: the pragmatist who wants to understand what benefit will come out of this. She is interested in the applications and implications. She is a practical experiential learner, who wants to know "so what? and what if?"

Each "person" will be reminding us to address their perspective (here not only in the book, but also in life) and also will periodically offer their personal summary.

Part 1 addresses a fundamental question on the mind of many educators: *Why do we need a change?* Delving into our current pedagogical approaches, and reflecting on how they match the audience and the times we live in, we will then explore what business schools can (and need to) learn from business. Finally, we will propose what may be the biggest turning point in the educative process: going from teaching to facilitating learning.

Part 2 introduces an approach to learning that was developed in Scandinavia. The methodology, called Action Reflection Learning™, has been used across the globe in designing and facilitating the learning of adults. The 10 principles on which this learning methodology is based constitute a blend of andragogy, cybernetics, social learning, systems thinking, behavioral, humanistic, and positive psychology. The description of each principle includes its rationale, the theoretical framework supporting the principle, a few stories with examples of exercises or processes that implement the principle, and considerations about the impact we can achieve by using each principle in the educational process.

Part 3 addresses the impact or consequences of such a different approach in responsible management education. It posits, what are the new roles of the teacher? What is the main goal of the educator in this context? What are the impacts of centering on the learner? The reader will find some examples of new ways of addressing higher education, examples that can be viewed as "out of the box" thinking. They do not focus on incremental change. They are concerned with radical transformation, with revolutionary new ways that we may not yet dream of, but ways that are actually happening already.

Finally, the Appendix presents a checklist of questions to aid educators in designing engaging learning experiences using the 10 principles.

What This Book Is Not

Higher education, and particularly the industry of business schools, is undergoing great pressures and considerable transformation.[3] Increased local and global competition, new nonuniversity competitors coming from consulting firms, such as Deloitte University and McKinsey Academy, online offerings, Massive Open Online Courses (MOOCs), increasing costs, diminishing returns or endowments, pressure to accommodate more students—all these factors combined make for a complex challenge. By presenting principles and tools that can be used for developing responsible managers in business schools, this book is not conditioning the framing of ideas and principles to the challenges of economic or structural constraints of the institutions. In other words, if the business model of higher education is exerting pressure to adapt teaching methods to an economic model that can provide an educational service within existing profitability boundaries, and if the question is "How can we have the largest number of students at the lowest cost and provide the best quality education?"—then this book provides neither solutions nor answers.

What the reader will find in this book is, however, an approach that responds to a different question: How can we develop in the most effective way a generation of responsible managers, who are able to take our civilization to an evolutionary breakthrough to shape a world that is sustainable, or even better, in terms of John Ehrenfeld,[4] that is flourishing for all? The return on investment (ROI), ultimately, may be not be measured only in dollars; it may be measured also in purpose, resilience, innovation, collaboration, entrepreneurship, in shaping a world that works for all. Certainly these other aspects can be monetized too, and they should, because their absence bears a cost we all ultimately pay. The perspective presented in the pages to follow is the pedagogical input: how learning happens best.

PART 1

Why Do We Need a Change?

CHAPTER 1

Pedagogy Frozen in Time

Some time ago, I came across an oil painting featuring a classroom. Desks were lined up in rows, and students were sitting facing the blackboard, their papers scattered on their desks. Some concentrated on their notebooks, others were looking over someone else's shoulder, one was daydreaming, and another was holding his head, immersed in his own worries, assuming from the expression on his face. The painting was titled *The Children's Class*, by French artist Henri Jules Jean Geoffroy, dated 1889.

The image struck me as I was amazed at its similarity with many of today's classrooms, particularly in higher education. Although some changes started especially in Masters and Executive Education in Europe, most higher education classrooms still have rows of tables lined up facing the white- or green-board, while some, more modern, are in a semicircle, amphitheater style. Of course, modern technology has entered the classroom, with projectors hanging somewhere from the ceiling, a Wi-Fi Internet connection, and button-operated screens that easily roll down and up. But other things remain very similar: some students are checking messages on their portable devices, while others are daydreaming or immersed in their own worries. "Nothing more challenging than undergrads," observed a colleague recently, concerned with the difficulty of getting his audience engaged. "They are just not interested in learning," another commented sadly and resignedly, while a third shared that he has a similar challenge even with graduates. He has taken to requiring them to switch off phones at the beginning of the class, in the attempt to get the students' undivided attention. Possible? Does this sound familiar to you?

It is true that many things have evolved in the way we teach children— with classrooms being far more dynamic today than the one portrayed in the painting: in many schools, students gather around small group tables, real life is brought into the room through their stories and news, project work makes learning fun and experiential, and technology helps the technology-natives find resources in a self-directed learning approach. Unfortunately, change has come slower in the higher levels of education.[1]

One reason for this is the different type of preparation undergone by instructors working in higher education. While school teachers earn their qualifying degrees by extensively studying pedagogy, business schools and higher education institutions in general count on instructors who are expert professionals in their own domain, many of whom step into academia with the aim of enriching their professional knowledge or experience with scholarly research. This can be traced back to the origins of the business school in this country. The first MBA program was designed in the United States in 1900, at the Dartmouth College's Tuck School of Business, with instructors recruited from among practicing or retired corporate managers who were hired to share with students their experience in the workplace. By midcentury, one could discern a trend in institutions becoming more research focused and less work oriented. Not for long though, since there arose a new crisis in the 1970s, when a study by the Carnegie Commission reported that business schools lacked relevance in their research topics, had an overly quantitative orientation, and did not prepare the young for entrepreneurial careers. This brought some changes in the course contents, although the pedagogical approach continued its expert-driven stance, which focused on lecturing for assimilation by the students.[2]

Undoubtedly, the lecture-based approach was the preferred learning style for some students, those who like to learn from experts, take notes, and memorize facts or be entertained and inspired by the particular life experience or knowledge of the instructor. There are others who prefer to learn by doing; who are interested in questioning data but feel intimidated to ask the "expert"; who seek to identify patterns, to learn by discovery; or are pragmatic and want to understand how the information would relate to their world. These types of learner may have more challenges to stay engaged.

The question arises: Who is our audience when we are standing in the front of the room? Are they technology-natives, who have short attention spans, who grew up bombarded by multiple and rapidly changing stimuli? Are they used to find the information they need with a touch of their screens, to type half words, to browse and surf at a speed we cannot follow? Are they comfortable receiving 140 characters, rather than listening to a person talking for 14 minutes? Can they even stay focused that long on something that is not totally exciting for them? At the same time, aren't they the ones who don't calculate how much time they are investing in something they feel passionate about, the ones who can work throughout the night without thinking of sleep deprivation if they are engaged in their task, and interacting with friends? Are they the ones who don't think of money, but of passion when it comes to work on a project they love?

At the turn of the millennium, Facebook didn't exist—today it has 1.5 billion monthly active users; mobile cellular subscriptions phone users grew from 738 million globally in 2000 to more than 7 billion by the end of 2015, according to the International Communications Union, the Geneva-based United Nations agency for communications and the official source for global statistics; YouTube didn't exist before 2005, and the first iPhone was invented in June 2007. Launched in 2006, Twitter accounted by the final quarter of 2016 an average of 307 million people actively microblogging monthly. The Chinese chat app Wechat grew in three years from zero to 639 million users, and the new chat and messaging Viber has close to 700 million registered users. How these technological changes transformed and shaped our lives is clearly seen in our day-to-day experiences. We all are journalists, moviemakers, and activists with just a "click"; we can learn what we are curious about with a screen touch, from anywhere. We share and disseminate information at the speed of light; we know we can reach almost anyone on this planet with a little research. Teenagers start nonprofits, school children launch campaigns for what they care about. It is then incomprehensible that we are spending hours and efforts[3] to inculcate information from the front of the classroom, to rows of individuals invited to sit and listen, so they can memorize and recite it back in a test.

The traditional expert-driven approach tends to be one-directional, with the instructor presenting and answering occasional questions. This approach is however increasingly eroded by the widespread access to information by anyone with a portable device. In a matter of seconds, any single piece of information that the lecturer presents can be updated, corrected, or completed with richer details. This is changing the power structure in the classroom. It has happened to many of us—to pause in midsentence trying to recall the exact title of a book, only to be helped out by a student who typed three letters into her phone and gave the exact reference. Not that we asked for it—we were just pausing to remember ... .

What is our role, then? What is the value that instructors are bringing, and from whose perspective is this judged? Has our hard-earned expertise built a pedestal from where we can talk and be respected? How tall is that pedestal? Is it so tall that we have difficulty hearing and seeing who is in the audience?

CHAPTER 2

What Business Schools Can Learn from Business

I must confess I bring a certain bias in my perspective, which originates in some decades working first as a therapist, and then as a trainer and coach in the corporate world. As a therapist, I learned to listen before talking, and to ask questions to jointly identify with the patient what we should work on, to help the patient take ownership of his process by introducing occasional challenging questions, and to expand his or her thinking. Later, as an external contractor for coaching and leadership development in the corporate world, I learned to address a potential client with what is called the "consultative selling" approach. When entering a meeting with a prospective client, the automatic expectation was that I would first articulate my experience and skills, and then tell him or her what they needed to do to address their challenges. However, to the surprise of the prospects, this was not the path I chose. Instead, I began by establishing a trusting, personal relationship, creating a safe space for our conversation. Then, I asked what the current needs or challenges were, how they were addressing them, or what they thought would help them to address those needs. Only after this would I assess what I might contribute that could be of value, and I would make an offer that our work together would become a codesigned intervention, where both parties influence the outcome. It was not about selling *a service*, it was about selling to *a person* a service.

When the contract for the intervention was assigned, my next task as a coach was to work with the employees. But how to ensure that what the person in the HR department thought was needed would in fact be relevant to, and needed by, the individuals concerned? Building on my previous practice as a therapist, I had learned all too well that many parents ask the therapist to help their children with a particular issue; the trouble was that usually what the parents had "diagnosed" was not relevant to the children's issues!

In a similar way, it became part of my corporate practice to contact the individuals who would be participating in the development sessions to discuss their personal challenges, needs, and developmental goals. In other words, they were invited to become owners of their learning, by codesigning or influencing the contents and goals of their developmental process. This step created the highest engagement levels, which were a good foundation for any program. I learned the importance of establishing a trusting, personal relationship, and creating a safe space for all the participants. It was not about developing generic skills, it was about developing needed skills of specific individuals. Now, what happens to be my preferred personal approach to the challenge actually corresponds to the development industry's best practices. Consultants know that their contract will only be renewed if their clients—the participants—give them a positive evaluation, if they find the intervention worth their time and the corporation's financial investment. Participants have no obligations or compromises to bias their feedback: It is provided to the HR division, and they can speak as honestly as they choose to about the value they experienced.

This client–service provider relationship in corporate training keeps practitioners on their toes, alert to what their participants may need, and drives the agenda of the most successful development professionals as they learn to stay flexible and adaptive to the organic needs of their clients in the room.

Interestingly, the principles of adult learning are currently observed more in a corporate setting than in a business school setting. Why is this so, what is the difference, and is there something that business schools can learn from business?

The first difference is in the power relation. A contracted trainer or coach is providing a paid service to a client and his performance will be measured by client satisfaction, effectiveness, usefulness, and perceived value added of the intervention. On the surface, this is not different from the educational setting: an instructor in a university is hired and paid for bringing his or her expertise and knowledge to students, who will fill in an evaluation form at the end of the term. The instructor's supervisor will hold periodic conversations about the professor's performance, and in a world of diminishing tenured positions, it may impact the instructor's permanence on the job.

However, something else happens in parallel. The instructor in a given subject defines what the learning outcomes will be, selects the contents that students will have to master, and to his or her best knowledge finds ways to accomplish this. The instructor also informs how the mastery or knowledge will be assessed, and what will determine if the student passes or fails. The rules are set by the instructor and the institution, and the students are expected to observe them.

These differing characteristics have a number of consequences. To begin with, they are establishing a different power relationship, where the instructor is still the validated authority in charge of the teaching process. However, the learning process becomes the responsibility of the student, and the instructor will be the one to assess if and how well the student has learned. In other words, teaching is decoupled from learning, something that is different in the corporate training world, where the trainer is responsible for teaching in a way that creates the desired learning, and where the trainer's performance will be measured by that. Teaching becomes the means by which to achieve the learning, not a goal in itself.

Students in a classroom often act in accordance with this polarized relationship, some by trying to get out of obligations whenever possible, some by assessing what is the minimum required (which can mean the minimum effort to get an A, because who needs an A+?), which are actions that embody the us-versus-you relationship. What do we (students) need to do to please, to conform, to get a good grade? What does the instructor want me to say, not say, memorize, quote? While many graduate students enroll with a passion for development and learning, the system tends to roll passion back into the lanes of "meeting what is expected" to pass, to get the necessary grades, and to graduate.

Certainly no educator has the intention to take the passion out of the equation and to convert the teaching–learning relationship into a pull-push, me-versus-you connection, driven by compliance in lieu of self-motivation. But it is an asymmetrical relationship, and this is widely accepted as a fact. The rules of the game indicate that, once enrolled in a course, it is no longer about what the learner wants, it is about what the instructor indicates has to be covered, and how. This leads to another undesirable consequence, which is the student's lack of ownership of the learning. When students have no such ownership, it becomes a challenge for the instructor to engage them. Many instructors struggle and try out different techniques and tricks to generate excitement in the students, with varied degrees of success.

A further complication is that the way the relationship is set up doesn't always go against the will of the students, who play their role in accepting the more passive position—waiting to be entertained, expecting the instructor to fill the airspace with contents and lectures, while comfortably remaining silent, letting him or her run "the show."

But it does not have to be this way.

CHAPTER 3

From Teaching to Facilitating Learning

When the same students sitting in a business school classroom participate in a training session at their corporation nowadays, there is evidence that they may be engaged in a very different way.

They may, for instance, be invited to identify their personal learning goals, and even in more traditional training settings they are invited to periodically assess how well the training is working for them, providing feedback, and in some cases voting with their feet by not showing up. The best development programs are tailored to the realities and defined needs of the individual, rather than being based on a generic list of desirable skills and behaviors. Needs assessments and surveys or organizational diagnostics may be conducted for trainers to understand the organization and the challenges the participants are facing. Trainers and coaches may study the corporate business strategy and how the individuals' performance could support it better; they may connect the contents of the training sessions with scorecards, performance reviews, 360° instruments, and developmental goals of the individuals involved. The best coaches and trainers design their sessions bearing in mind the different learning styles of the participants, and they pay constant attention to the levels of energy in the room. In good corporate development programs, the teaching and learning are mutually reinforcing; they are not decoupled as in our educational institutions, and they are both considered the responsibility of both the instructor and the participants.

While this may seem to place the burden of responsibility exclusively on the trainer and relieve the student of any accountability for growth, in actuality the opposite occurs. When the student is relieved of the obligation to comply with the expectations of the instructor, ownership of the process ceases to be that of the teacher. Who owns the process then? As if a ball were tossed in the air that the instructor does not catch, then students automatically might tend to catch it. When students realize that they are not studying and performing "for the instructor," they begin to realize that they are the central beneficiaries of their learning. As a result, the learner's accountability increases significantly. Or the participant lets the ball drop and doesn't show up.

A Story

Some years ago I was teaching a Change Management course at the MBA in the University of Belgrano, Buenos Aires. At the first session I asked students what they would need from me, how they would like this course to be run. After some minutes of puzzlement, they began to state expectations like "don't lecture," "make it interactive," "have dialogues," "make it real." I accepted the request, and proposed that they would read certain materials, and we would use the sessions to explore reactions, questions, their perspectives on what they read, and how it related to an ongoing change project they would manage in their organization. Everyone liked the idea.

All went well—for a few weeks. Then one class as I entered the room there was an unusual silence. As I asked the question: What did you think about the reading this week? I couldn't catch the eyes of anyone. They were looking at their papers, out the window, at their fingers. I asked them what was happening, and after exchanging some looks among them, one student spoke up. "What happened is that this week we had a lot of work for mid-term from the other courses. And the other professors are not like you ... ." Without inquiring what that meant, I reflected for a moment and made another offer. Look, we agreed on doing it this way because it was what you asked for. But it may not be realistic, and it may not fit your needs, so moving forward I am willing to come with prepared lectures.

There was a silence in the room. After a few moments, another student spoke up.

I don't know if others agree with me, Professor, but I think we are just not used to this. We have all had 16 years of educational experience where the teachers told us what to do, and how, and when. This is different. You are asking us to decide, to take responsibility for what we want to learn, and we can influence the how. I think we're just not used to it. Would you give us another chance, to try it out for a few more weeks?

He looked around the room and others were nodding in agreement. That is what we did. I explained again that I was there to serve their needs, to help them learn, and that how we did it was something that we could periodically revisit and change. Needless to say, they all read and participated from there on until the end of the semester.

Professional instructors design their sessions with the learning outcomes in mind, and apply principles of adult learning to make the experience more powerful and effective. That means that the participants are invited to influence the design and contents to best suit their context and learning needs. This is the cornerstone of ownership of the learning process. The role of the instructor changes, and he or she becomes more focused on facilitating learning.

Learning facilitation is an approach to development that is particularly suited for responsible management education. Responsible management education[1] is defined as the preparation and development of individuals to address the complex planetary challenges. Different authors include in this the ability to shape a better world, to restore the earth's resources, to address the developmental goals for a sustainable world as defined by the United Nations Global Compact.[2] Given the size of our challenge, all the different professional disciplines will be called to address the problems from their particular technical perspective (engineering, technology, strategy, finance, accounting, marketing, law, social sciences, health sciences, urban planning, agricultural sciences, etc.). Yet, there is more than technical knowledge involved in developing responsible management.

Scholarly research about the knowledge, skills, and competencies that responsible management calls for has identified aspects related to a host of different content areas: ecoliteracy,[3] systems thinking,[4] scenario planning, complexity theory,[5] change management, ethics,[6] emotional intelligence, spiritual intelligence,[7] leadership,[8] stakeholder theory,[9] collaborative practices,[10] contemplative practices,[11] creativity and innovation,[12] social entrepreneurship. These content areas shape and inform a particular way of thinking, being, and acting in the world, and are core to the responsible management we need for our world—independent of the manager's professional orientation.

Responsible management education therefore is not limited to an intellectual understanding of the contents, the challenges, and opportunities, but instead demands a holistic engagement of the individual: it touches the values, the identity, the purpose, the assumptions and beliefs, the habits, the sense of self, and even the soul.[13]

This kind of development requires the full presence of the participants, meaning not just their physical presence in the room, but also a presence with all their senses and all their being. More than a cognitive exercise of the mind, educators are tasked with fostering an integral development of the individuals. This is when it becomes clear that the traditional approach to teaching, so common in our business schools, has become inadequate. We cannot teach values, there are no formulas to calculate a person's purpose; we cannot test the student's understanding of what will make them responsible change agents. Independently of the context and contents we are teaching, there is a component that relates not to facts and data, but to making meaning out of the whole learning experience. And this is when we need to bring back the passion, to foster accountability for the results. We need the full person in the room.[14]

In this section, we have seen that our audience in the classroom has dramatically changed. The purpose of education also changed, if we think that our most important priority is bringing this planet back into sustainability—or even shaping a world that for once is flourishing for all. We need to develop empowered individuals who can drive creative change. As the Principle #3 wisely anticipated it, for responsible management education, we need new learning methods and tools.[15] Given the urgency to act, we need to stop teaching lessons, and to start facilitating learning for students.

In the next section, we will introduce ten learning principles for facilitating learning, and where they originated.

PART 2

What Is Action Reflection Learning?

CHAPTER 4

The Scandinavian Rebels' Initiative

In the late 1970s, a group of academics, consultants, and corporate managers came together in the south of Sweden to address a topic of common concern. The group felt that the way managers were being developed in business schools was not adequately preparing them for the demands of corporate life. They thought that the business world needed better-prepared leaders, not simply managers. The business school curricula abounded in theory about strategic planning, financial management, administration of personnel, and plant operations, but lacked a meaningful syllabus preparing students for successful leadership. Graduate programs were preparing managers, not leaders.[1] In a constructivist mode, they put together elements that seemed to work, independently of the theories behind them, and designed the first leadership program. It was a program for corporate managers who came together for a week at a time, over a period of several months, with the task of solving a real organizational challenge, one in which they had no expertise at all. A "project team advisor" accompanied the group as they worked together, providing just-in-time support through tools, questions, or resources to help the group make progress on the task and to learn at the same time. The program was designed using elements of action learning, modified by the active role of the project team advisor (coach).

After running several programs, in 1981, a group selected the most innovative leadership development institutions in the United States, and visited them to discover new ways of developing leaders. They visited top management educational institutions in Boston (Boston Consulting Group, Harvard, MIT), New York (American Management Association, Aspen Institute, New York University, Tarrytown Executive Conference Center), Tucson (Motorola Institute, University of Arizona), Northern

California (Esalen Institute, Hewlett-Packard, Stanford University, University of California at Berkeley), and Los Angeles (UCLA, University of Southern California).[2] It soon became a two-way learning experience, where they shared their new approach with a very interested audience. After this trip, they distilled their findings, and concluded that indeed a vastly different approach to development was needed—one that would not be centered on the lectures of experts, but which developed leaders who could thrive on change, learn to be comfortable with ambiguity and uncertainty, and who could build trusting relationships and learn by action and reflection. This approach would acknowledge the existence of the past experience and of the tacit knowledge of the participants, accepting that they were no tabula rasa; the classroom would be used as a meeting place for surfacing diversity of experience and input, and a point would be made to challenge the mental models and beliefs of the participants. They considered it essential to go beyond the traditional focus on logic and rational thinking; they invited the inclusion of feelings, of intuition and right brain hemisphere inputs, as a way of engaging not only the intellect but also the whole person.[3] The arena for learning would be real-life challenges instead of case studies and theories, and the participants would be made actors of their own learning.

Since this approach centered on taking action to address a real challenge, on the importance of extracting learning by reflecting on the experience, and on the power of individuals owning their learning, the U.S.-based sister organization LIM suggested calling this approach "Action Reflection Learning."[4]

What characterized this group of pioneering practitioners was that they felt free of academic constraints. Their main focus was on how managers could learn best, not on the institutional or theoretical boundaries prescribing how learning had to be designed and implemented. Corporate facilitators, Organizational Development professionals, and trainers from the United States and other countries, even some university professors with an exploratory spirit, joined the movement, adding their experiences with participants of different ethnicities, nationalities, language, and cultures. Over the following decades, practitioners around the globe experimented with new Action Reflection Learning (ARL)-based designs tailored to a variety of adult learning needs, such as developing leaders, cross-functional teams, innovation teams, crisis teams, high-performance teams, or developing HR as business partners. Today, it is also used for individual coaching, to design meetings or stand-alone workshops, conference presentations, and university courses, combining different elements and interventions that can bring about profound learning.[5] A common trait among ARL practitioners is their pragmatism: They value what works, rather than what theories suggest, which gives the conceptual freedom to use behaviorist and humanist approaches at the same time, although the scholarly frameworks are different and even contradict each other. This experimental approach could have been called trial and learning (as opposed to the classic trial and error), as each new situation becomes an opportunity to learn what worked and what could be done differently for a better outcome.

Unintentionally, the ARL practitioners shaped a learning methodology based on various bodies of research: cybernetics, social learning, systems thinking, action learning, transformational learning, behaviorism, humanistic psychology, philosophy, andragogy, and experiential learning. It must be noted that the practitioners were not seeking to put theories in practice; they were in many cases averse to theories, or at best, interested in developing their own theories, but, at the same time, they accepted that different conceptual frameworks could be equally valid, and could coexist. Many also considered that when a theory becomes the accepted explanation of something, the growth of knowledge stagnates, freezing pieces of reality into conceptual boxes, and conditioning behaviors to remain within the accepted boundaries, and therefore becomes an obstacle to innovation and creative experimentation.

This was the reason that the ARL approach remained somehow underresearched and little known for several decades, despite its documented powerful impact on learning. The DNA of the approach was that it shouldn't be cast in bronze, and there was a shared understanding that ARL was what a practitioner could make out of it, without an authoritative definition of what ARL is and what it is not.

At the same time, this fluid condition made the transfer and evolution of knowledge extremely challenging, and limited the development of new practitioners who wanted to "learn ARL." In 2005, an initiative was launched to code the methodology,[6] comparing the existing practices of ARL and identifying the commonalities among the approaches. As a result of this research, a number of common elements were found and 10 underlying learning principles were identified, to which the power of the ARL approach can be attributed.

The urgency of our planetary challenges demands innovative action, entrepreneurship, and proactive individuals who can work with a new paradigm of leadership—one that is inclusive, and collaborative, that fosters creativity, and that operates by keeping the welfare of this and the future generations. We need empowered individuals across the globe, who can act with compassion and intelligence and with cognitive, emotional, and spiritual intelligence. We need a multitude of young minds inspired by their highest values, by their passion and conviction that they can shape a better world for all. Fortunately, isolated experiments[7] have shown that we have these new leaders sitting in our classrooms, just bored and waiting for the invitation to be part of something greater. In the following chapters, we will introduce the 10 learning principles[8] of ARL, an eclectic methodology to facilitate their learning as they emerge as responsible managers.

CHAPTER 5

The 10 ARL Principles

This following chapters introduce the 10 Action Reflection Learning™ (ARL) principles. Each principle is introduced with its rationale, the theoretical framework supporting it, a few stories with examples of exercises or processes for implementing the principle, and considerations about the impact we can achieve through its implementation.

In any audience we have individuals with different learning style preferences. Bernice McCarthy,[1] who based her work on David Kolb's model,[2] describes the four learning styles in simple terms:

1. The Why learners
2. The What learners
3. The How learners
4. The So What—What if learners

The Why learners want to primarily understand why a certain topic is important before they can grant any attention to it. The What learners, in turn, do not give that much importance to why a topic is important, but are more interested in what the topic is about: definitions, rationale, studies supporting it, data, and facts. The How learners are motivated by understanding how the session (or exercise, or process) will flow. They want instructions, or indications of what will happen in the class. They want to get involved in action if possible, and are not seduced by theories or rationales. Finally, the So What—What if learners' first questions are "What will this session's take away be for me? How will I be able to use the information? What difference will it make to know it?" They are the ultimate pragmatists, and they need to start with the final goal in mind. While we all have a combination of preferences, there is frequently one that is stronger than the others. Considering the learning preferences distributed in the room, a presenter should always spend the first minutes addressing briefly the four questions—Why? What? How? So What? This simple strategy will ensure that he captures the attention of the whole audience, who may then be engaged and ready to listen to what follows.

Following this concept, this section has been written with the four learning styles in mind, addressing the "why, what, how and so what questions" of the readers.

As we go through the 10 principles, we will see how each principle can be made relevant and accessible to each of the four styles.

She is the voice of the Why learner, who asks, Why is this important? Why should I care about it?

Julia

Voice of the What learner, who asks, What is the definition of the topic? Its rationale? What are the data and facts? What is the theory supporting it?

Nick

Voice of the How learner, who asks, How can we apply what we are discussing? How can we find out how this works? How to bring theory into the classroom?

Andres

Voice of the So What learner, who asks, What will come out of this? What are its practical applications? What are the implications for the future? The benefits?

Vivien

They will be reminding us to address their perspective, and also will periodically offer their personal summary.

The 10 Action Reflection Learning principles

Relevance	Paradigm shift
Tacit knowledge	Systems thinking
Reflection	Integral
Self-awareness	Repetition and reward
Social learning	Learning facilitator

CHAPTER 6

Principle 1: Relevance

One ought to demand nothing of children through obedience ... they can learn nothing of which they do not feel the real and present advantage in either pleasure or utility .... Present interest, that is the great mover, the only one which leads surely and far.

—Jean-Jacques Rousseau

Definition

Learning is optimal when the focus of the learning is owned by, important, and timely for the individual.[1]

Julia: Why should a lesson be relevant?

Think of how you learned to talk. You were barely three years old, and you had learned a number of words that helped you to communicate and express your needs and wishes. How did you learn the syntax and complexity of your own language, without any structured lessons? You learned because you were highly motivated by your needs. Words became tickets to get what you wanted, and you were ready to adopt them. The situation was fully relevant for you. Now compare how you learned a foreign language, or mathematical equations. It may have been based on effort, will, persistence, or discipline.

The same happens hundreds of times every day. When we think of learning, we tend to picture a classroom or a piano lesson. However, most of our learning is organic, and happens in the moment in unstructured ways: we learn when listening to the news, when reading signs on the highway, when we overhear a conversation, when we read the instructions and warnings listed on a medication, when we try to figure out a new appliance, from asking questions of others, even asking Siri or Google.

And that learning is powerful: we are focused, engaged, and we will easily incorporate and use the new information we have "learned." In informal, unstructured ways, we are constantly scanning the environment and learning what is relevant for us in the moment. Effortless. Why not use the same principle that makes these learning moments possible, and apply it in the classroom? Can't we all imagine how a classroom would be if the students found high relevance in all they are doing, or what we are sharing!?

Nick: But what exactly does relevance mean?

Relevance means that something matters to someone. In the educational context that we are focusing on here—the development of responsible managers—it means that each student in the room should feel a personal connection to what is being discussed or presented—because he sees it related to his life, work, values, concerns, future, dilemmas, challenges, or opportunities.

This is not a new concept. For almost a century this principle has been present in all learner-centered approaches. At the same time, in the more traditional (and unfortunately still prevalent) teacher-centered approach, the expert plays the main role, deciding what the students need to know, how they need to know it, and also how the expert evaluates their understanding.[2] Brazilian educator Paulo Freire called this the "banking approach," using the analogy of an instructor making deposits of information into the minds of the students.[3]

Nick: If scholars have known for so long that the learner-centric approach is better, why is it not widespread?

The endurance of this approach to education across time and geography may be related to the predominance of the patriarchal model, according to educator Riane Eisler.[4] She defines the domination (patriarchal) model and compares it with the partnership model.[5] In the mostly prevalent domination model, one side seeks to maintain control and power over the other. This can be found in racial, religious, family, gender, tribal, socioeconomic, geopolitical, ethnic, and even cultural settings. The partnership model, by contrast, is found in certain small communities, such as Gaviotas in Colombia,[6] in long-lasting civilizations such as the Minoan in Central Europe, in the community of Ladakh in northern India,[7] or the Mindanao in the Philippines, to name a few. They organize their society around the inhabitants' individual skills and strengths, and not around hierarchical power structures, functioning therefore as collaborative societies. They still have conflicts, but manage them in different ways, not with one party overpowering the other.

Although these are only a handful of examples of the well-enacted partnership model, there is undoubtedly a worldwide tendency away from patriarchal models. We can observe it in the progressive democratization of nations; the growth of women's rights; the cultural disapproval of ethnic, racial, or other discrimination; and the collapse of dictatorships. It may be just the beginning phase, but we are observing a global shift toward a partnership model.[8]

The learner-centered approach corresponds to a partnership model of relationship. In this approach, the student plays an active role that can range from codesigning a session with the instructor, to influencing the contents and the methods, to fully identifying what she wants or needs to learn, and how she will learn it.

Nick: Isn't this what andragogy proposed?

Certainly. Malcolm Knowles[9] in the 1970s studied the differences between teaching children and teaching adults, coining the term "andragogy" to refer to a self-directed learning approach, which he found more appropriate for adults. Andragogy suggests that adults can learn best when they use their experience, that they are motivated by improving their performance, and they show great readiness to learn. These characteristics are present in work-based learning,[10] where managers develop their skills by working on real work projects or challenges and by extracting learning from their experience in trying to solve them. In educational settings, a similar approach has been used more recently, under the name of problem-based learning or issue-centric learning, where students learn about a subject through the experience of solving an open-ended problem. What all these approaches have in common is the relevance factor: the learner is engaged and motivated because he perceives the challenge to have an actual bearing on his area of interest, his well-being, his professional growth, and it is of significance to his learning.

Before the concept of andragogy was developed, relevance was present at the foundation of experiential learning, an approach proposed at the turn of the 1900s by American educators John Dewey[11] and Eduard Lindeman.[12] Later, David Kolb,[13] among others, continued researching experiential learning. In experiential learning, the student becomes the one actively exploring a topic, delving deep into his own thoughts and experiences, and drawing inferences by himself rather than depending for insight on the input of the instructor ("the sage on stage"). Other adult learning scholars have developed research and practices centered on this approach, where individuals use a current situation or experience as the arena for more relevant learning, under the names of situated learning,[14] action research,[15] inquiry learning,[16] self-managed learning,[17] and action learning.[18]

Andres: Well, the theory is interesting, but how can relevance be brought into a classroom?

There are multiple ways to bring relevance into the classroom. To begin with, we can make a session relevant if we know the context, concerns, questions, interests, and curiosity of the learners. As educators, we shouldn't assume what these are, but find out what they are.

There are three simple ways to bring this principle of relevance to life.

- Fostering ownership of the learning
- Linking what is presented with their context or reality
- Providing just-in-time interventions, meaning waiting until the timing is right to introduce a concept, as opposed to sticking to a preplanned agenda

A Story

On one occasion I had been invited to give a special lecture to a group of students attending a class from a colleague. My colleague had suggested I reserve some minutes at the end of the lecture for questions, although he warned that his students may probably not ask many, if any. After the welcome and introduction, I announced the topic I would present, and asked the students to take one minute and identify one question they had related to the topic, and write it down. After they wrote their questions, I listened to them and grouped them by themes and spent the remaining time addressing those. This initial process ensured that the participants had an opportunity to develop some ownership of their own learning, and I noticed the audience was highly engaged.

Andres: But what if they don't know what they don't know?

This is a good point. Few people know all they need to about a topic, and some are aware that they have more to learn about it. However, they won't ask questions if they think they know "enough"—which is to say they will not find out what they don't know. Therefore, the instructor should be prepared to include content she thinks the audience could find of value, in addition to the topics the students requested. This will expand their understanding, and is called a *just in time* (JIT) *intervention*. The instructor has to stay attentive to the emerging questions or concerns, and use those moments as opportunities to make other JIT comments, since they ensure maximum relevance of the learning for the students.

Another way to help make learning relevant is by *linking* what is presented with the reality and context of the participants—for example, asking them how what is being presented could connect with their circumstances. This is a very important phase of the learning facilitation, since, when we introduce something that the students didn't know before, it is up to us to build the bridge between the new content and their reality. When we omit the step of linking contents to context, it will be easily forgotten by the students and become a waste of our and their time.

Vivien: So what are the positive impacts we can expect when paying attention to making a class relevant for the students?

The first visible impact will be heightened engagement. When the topic connects to something that is real and current to the audience, the participants are automatically engaged; they can see how it relates to their life or interests, they can link what they are learning to their contexts outside of the classroom. Throughout a typical day we rapidly focus on what is relevant to us, and we learn without effort how to get to a meeting, news about our neighborhood, information that impacts a project we are currently working on, and the list goes on. However, if we look at the subjects taught in our programs of higher education, what percentage of the content would you say has a clear link to the life or interests of the students?

A Story

In a course to develop the sustainability mindset, after presenting information about the state of the planet, I invited students to think of a possible project to make a difference in an area they felt passionate about—either because they loved it, or because they felt the urge to act upon it. They were given some time to reflect in silence, after which they presented their selected projects to make a difference. They grouped by similar interests and the key was that they selected something they felt excited about. As a result of this process one student later wrote in a post that having so many projects to do for all her current courses, this was the one project she cared about. It didn't feel it was work although they were investing more time than I had expected.

The relevance does not always have to be only in the content of the learning, but can also be in the process of learning. For example, learning to express oneself in writing or speaking is a skill that can become relevant if we allow the participants to find how valuable the competence of clear communication can be in the reality of their professional life.

Vivien: But how does relevance connect with shaping responsible managers?

The challenges of our time require that we combine logical, analytical thinking, and creative innovation. We are faced with problems caused by decisions that we made decades ago and by habits learned in our youth but continuing in the present time. We need to reinvent most of our behaviors ranging across a wide spectrum—how we buy and consume products, how we now travel, move merchandise, design products, even entertain ourselves and guests. This is a daunting task, something we have not experienced in the history of humanity, and, on top, it is urgent. However, we have the large unused potential of everyone's contribution to developing solutions and ideas. If we keep the instruction time disconnected from the reality of our students, we only will get their bare minimum attention—and for short time spans. Instead, when we link the contents we teach to the challenges and opportunities for shaping a better world, we make it relevant for them and their own future.

Andres: It is not clear to me how to make a session individually relevant when, let's say, there are 200 or more students in the classroom. Not many educators have the privilege of a small group.

Size matters certainly, but taking a moment to invite the audience to reflect and identify what they want to get out of a session can be a little gesture that makes a large difference. Even with a large group, everyone can be invited to take a silent moment and write down a question he or she personally wants to have answered, then one minute to exchange it with the person in the neighboring seat. This is a two-minute investment that helps the participants create some ownership for their learning, and to focus on what they want to get out of class, as opposed to sitting passively throughout. Fortunately new technologies like Poll Everywhere allow for instant input from the audience using their cell phones. And even if the facilitator or presenter is not able to hear all the questions, he can build in some time and ask the audience to look for their answers on their own on their portable devices or in a brief exchange with their neighbor, and address those that haven't been answered during the final section of the lecture. It is therefore important to reserve time for this, to invite the participants to go back to their initial question, and to check if it was answered—or if a new one emerged. By doing this, we are also conveying a strong message to the participants: That we want them to own their learning and influence the session. And when we do this, it is important to make our intention explicit, by explaining why we are asking them to identify their question. If educators assume that the best way to spend the time is filling it with a lecture they think the students need, then they shouldn't be surprised if that puts the audience into a passive frame of mind. The educational system has tended to induce this passivity, so by stating why we are inviting them to take ownership of their learning we help them become aware of a habit we urge them to break.

Planning a class schedule that provides time to reflect, to identify questions, and to hear and address them becomes more important than merely downloading content into the students' brains, since content is available in many user-friendly ways for anyone, 24/7. Focus on relevance also calls for educators to critically examine what of the content is not available otherwise to the participants, that is, personal experience, meaning making out of data, and then ensuring that we make it available to them.

Julia: Summarizing, relevance is the golden link that connects information with our own world. We have to find ways to create that link, checking with the audience.

Nick: It has been at the core of many adult learning theories. We learn faster and remember more what is relevant, current, and real for us.

Andres: Asking what do you want to know is a simple way to create ownership of the learning and only takes a moment; but also just-in-time contents may be ways to create relevance, and help students find how a new concept links with their world and reality.

Vivien: If we only could make each of our classes relevant to the students, we would hugely increase their engagement and unleash the intellectual potential of the future leaders in very creative ways.

CHAPTER 7

Principle 2: Tacit Knowledge

I didn't know I had any thoughts until I let my pen go. The pen knows more than I think!

—A participant

Definition

Knowledge exists within individuals in implicit forms of which the individual is unaware: it is under- or not fully utilized and can be accessed through guided introspection.

Nick: This principle reminds me of Socrates and the maieutic, he thought people already had all the knowledge and he just had to extract it via questions.

You are right. This principle is found throughout history, with perhaps the most quoted example being Socrates's method. We can also find it in the etymology of the Latin word "education," *educere* meaning to extract, literally "to lead out" or bring out something that is already latent within the person. The First Nation indigenous group of Unangan, which has been living for over 10,000 years in what are now the Aleutian Islands, which straddle the Pacific Ocean and the Bering Sea, does not use many words to transfer knowledge to their young. The Unangan consider that their children can be led, by means of short questions, to find the knowledge and wisdom within themselves. Similarly, we find in the roots of Zen Buddhism, and other spiritual or religious traditions, invitations to individuals to find the wisdom inside themselves, rather than in external sources of authority. The underlying assumption is that the answers to a person's questions already lie within themselves and are far more powerful or effective than those provided by others.

Nick: This sounds like the foundation of psychotherapies, too.

True. This principle has also been at the foundation of early studies of psychology (William James), psychoanalysis (Freud, Jung), and later psychotherapeutic methods: helping individuals uncover their own answers, expanding their consciousness by accessing their tacit knowledge or wisdom. Actually, the term "tacit knowledge" was first presented by Polanyi in 1958,[1] and later developed by Nonaka.[2] Tacit knowledge is not only an individual phenomenon, but it can also be found within a group or a community of practice,[3] where people act upon a knowledge that they cannot explain easily or readily put into words.

Julia: Tacit knowledge may be valuable in dealing with our soul or behaviors, but why is the students' tacit knowledge something important in a classroom when we know they are investing time and money to go to school in the search for new knowledge?

We can go back to the banking analogy proposed by Brazilian educator Paulo Freire.[4] According to Freire, when teachers share information and expect students to receive it, memorize, and repeat it, they are acting like a bank, where deposits are made, and employees receive, file, and store them. He questions this traditional way of understanding education, reminding us that the learner is never an empty vessel, a "tabula rasa." Children, and even more so adults, have accumulated information that shapes frameworks and mental models. This tacit body of knowledge conditions our interpretations and how we will incorporate any new information. If we stand in front of a classroom and see the students merely as empty containers to be filled with our precious information, we will be paying the price of misreading our audience. If we, instead, see the classroom as a gathering place for young people intent on active inquiry and exploring the new, we will open the space for a rich dialogue as we help them access their tacit knowledge.

Andres: I still cannot imagine how I could extract any tacit knowledge from students in, let's say, accounting practices or any STEM disciplines (science, technology, engineering, math).

That is a good point. As we saw before, there are things that we simply don't know. The tacit knowledge does not refer to those. It refers to what we don't know that *we know*. An easy process to implement this principle is to ask questions. Before starting with a lecture or introducing a concept, the instructor can ask an open question to the audience to help them bring up what they know.

A Tool

The best way to engage everyone in accessing what they don't know they know is a Stop Reflect Write Report.* In this process, the facilitator invites everyone to take a minute and write thoughts in response to a specific question. In any given group, there are individuals who need to reflect in silence, and others who develop their thoughts by talking (extroverts). This can create a delicate situation when we ask a question, because while the extroverts will readily give their perspective, the introverts have to decide whether to listen or to reflect, and mostly tend to listen and let others do the work. By asking everyone to write in silence during one minute, we help the extroverts edit their thoughts, and the introverts access their tacit knowledge. Then everyone can share their views, and contributions are multiplied, all in a fraction of the time it would take a group to respond to an open question without first reflecting on the replies.

Asking a question to the audience and inviting everyone to reflect is very different from a common (and unfortunate) habit that some instructors have when they ask the students to guess the end of a half sentence, such as "This approach is called ... ?"—and then looking around, wait for someone to guess what is on his mind. When a few students take the risk to complete the sentence, only to fail to provide the right answer, the instructor then gives the answer himself—"This approach is called ... *patronizing!*" This habit, albeit unintentionally, can create an atmosphere of disrespect for the students, who are reduced to mere guessers of the

---

* SRWR: A tool developed by LIM LLC, with permission.

expert's thread of thought. This is not a helpful way of using questions, and if we have ever been in such a situation, we know the mix of frustration and humiliation it can create. As Riane Eisler[5] would say, this is a common use of overpowering and exemplifies the domination model in action.

Another way to elicit the tacit knowledge that is in the room is for the educator to resist the urge to answer a question posed by the students, and to turn the question back to the group, for them to answer. It is surprising how many rich answers emerge from this broadened source of information, and it allows the instructor to probe their rationale, ask for clarification, support evidence, and eventually complement the responses with her own experience or answers. The key here is to resist the temptation to step into the self-rewarding role of the all-knowing expert.

Vivien: Help me understand how we are developing more responsible managers by bringing out the students' tacit knowledge.

Russ McDonald,[6] a professor from the University of Auckland in New Zealand, wrote an interesting book about a course to educate for responsibility in management. He found that students need to be given the opportunity to take ownership of their learning, by defining what they would like to see in a better world, what values would make that better world, and what new behaviors would be needed to support that change. McDonald holds back on his own experience or perspective, and instead he asks plenty of questions to prompt the students to reflect, to shape their own opinions, and to present them in well-constructed statements. This requires another condition, which he describes eloquently: The creation of a safe space, where students don't feel judged or ridiculed, but rather appreciated and stimulated in furthering their thinking. His approach is not limited however to ethics courses. Exploring the values we live by and those that would make this a better world is something embedded in any discipline, whether science, art, or humanities. Not even technology exists outside a framework of values. The big contribution of bringing out the tacit knowledge is not to fill out technical information, but rather (a) to explore existing beliefs, assumptions, and values and (b) to create a learning situation where the student is respected as a holder of valuable knowledge.

> *Julia: Summarizing, the principle of Tacit Knowledge means that students may know more than they think, and we can help them discover this.*
>
> *Nick: Yes, and that principle has been widely present in human civilization across time and cultures—we can find the underlying assumption in philosophy, religion, spiritual traditions, and psychotherapy, even in modern-day's coaching, if I may say so.*
>
> *Andres: It may not be applicable for situations when they just don't know. But when we think the students may have some tacit knowledge, we can ask a question and have everyone ponder over it. And resist answering the questions ourselves . . . .*
>
> *Vivien: We may develop more self-confident individuals, who learn to trust themselves all the while testing the strength of their perspectives by sharing them with their colleagues. Responsibility is developed from the inside out, and not taught from the outside.*

CHAPTER 8

Principle 3: Reflection

No one can see their reflection in running water. It is only in still water that we can see.

—Taoist Proverb

Definition

Reflection is the process of being able to thoughtfully ponder an experience, which can enable greater meaning and learning to be derived from a given situation.

Julia: This sounds like a very obvious part of everyday life. Why is it highlighted as a learning principle?

It may seem obvious, but in today's hectic lifestyle, with an increasing list of obligations that seldom get attended to, reflection is less a common habit than we would imagine. It's true, of course, that we all draw conclusions from almost everything that happens to us, and ask ourselves, Why did this happen? But many times, our conclusions are really hasty assumptions, forged with no deep scrutiny, and do not create real, valuable learning. To extract real learning from events and interactions, we need to slow down, pause, and reflect.

Nick: Are you referring to the philosophical understanding of reflection?

Philosophers have definitely evidenced reflection as the best method to deepen our understanding; witness the Greek thinkers Socrates, Plato, and Aristotle. For them and others, reflection has constituted an essential method to gain wisdom. Plato asked: "... why should we not calmly and patiently review our own thoughts, and thoroughly examine and see what these appearances in us really are?" More recently, educator John Dewey[1] was the first to signal the key role of reflection in the learning process. David Kolb,[2] elaborating further on Dewey's experiential learning concept, developed a learning cycle of four linked phases; of which, reflection was one. The four phases are: concrete experience (the action itself); reflective observation (to critically reflect upon and investigate the experience); abstract conceptualization (meaning to develop ideas and hypotheses); and active experimentation (when based on our ideas and hypotheses, we take action in the world). This was influenced by Kurt Lewin's process of Action Research,[3] characterized by continuous cycles of action and reflection to test hypotheses and create new knowledge in the area of social sciences. Chris Argyris's[4] theory of single- and double-loop learning is also based on reflection. If we are able to identify the assumptions that underpin our behaviors, we can revise them and extract lessons for other situations. This was elaborated further by Kegan and Lahey, who pointed at the importance of identifying the "big assumption" behind our beliefs and actions.[5]

Vivien: Does this mean that reflection is an important principle for responsible management education because individuals are able to analyze their behaviors?

Yes, this is a core step in our personal development journey of becoming responsible citizens of the planet in these demanding times. A school of thought called "critical reflection"[6] has proposed the power of reflection to question truths, structures, and distribution of power, as well as to increase the understanding of self. For the adult education scholar and educator Stephen Brookfield,[7] four activities are central to critical reflection:

a. Assumption analysis: We need to challenge our beliefs, values, cultural practices, and social structures in order to assess their impact on our daily behaviors;

b. Contextual awareness: We will discover how our assumptions are socially and personally created in a specific historical and cultural context;

c. Imaginative speculation: Then we can start thinking in new ways about the same phenomena; and

d. Reflective skepticism: We need to maintain a constant practice of questioning what could be presented as universal truths.

Critical reflection has also been elevated to the primary objective of adult education in the work of Jack Mezirow,[8] who views it as essential to help students go through transformative learning.

As you can see, reflection is not only about understanding the self, but also about our context, and about developing a habit of questioning and revising what is taken for granted. This is critical to bring about the changes we need.

Andres: Can you give us a few examples or techniques for integrating reflection into the classroom?

Reflecting on an event or an action allows us to detach ourselves from the situation, and to establish a "reflecting subject" or "scrutinized event-object" dynamic. In order to be able to revise our behaviors and our experiences to extract lessons, the first condition is to pause. If we jump from one action to the next, there is no time to process and ponder what actually happened, and why. The instructor needs therefore to be aware of his own pace, and make time to extract meaning from the events. The pause and invitation to reflect can take place both inside the classroom, as well as through assignments between sessions.

A Story

Students around the globe are living under a lot of pressure, taking several courses, keeping up with the assignments, sometimes carrying a job, having a family, dealing with romance, maintaining their social relationships, making time for service hours to add points to their resume, and forging their identity, to name a few. All this fosters short attention spans, forces the students to attempt to multitask, which results in them being reduced to giving little attention to many tasks. How do we get them to pause?

One activity I have used is called The Coffee Shop. The assignment asks them to find a coffee shop and sit there for 45 minutes, leaving their phone in the office or at home. With nothing to write or read. Just plain sit there. If thoughts come about what they could be doing, what they just did or still have to do, they should notice them, and let them pass, because the assignment is just to sit there, and doing nothing is not only fine, but also is the point of the exercise.

This is one of the most powerful exercises, and as they get back, students write down and post a wealth of thoughts that indicate a profound time they just spent with themselves. This simple exercise helps them experience the power of pausing, noticing the pace of their daily life, realizing how many useless thoughts occupy our mind, and how many valuable reflections can emerge from quietness.

Questions are a great tool to foster reflection, and they should be open, nonleading questions. They can be probing and challenging. Silent individual reflection time, writing down thoughts in a learning journal, and using the Stop-Reflect-Write-Report tool to share an edited version of our thoughts are a few ways to develop the habit of reflection. Skillfully selected questions can guide students to extract clear meaning from events and discussions, to clarify how something relates to their life; questions can lead to exploration of feelings and assumptions, and also help students to imagine scenarios, anticipate, visualize, and plan.

Andres: Summarizing then, to bring the powerful principle of reflection into our classrooms we need first to slow ourselves down, to make space to ask questions, and allow students the time to silently reflect—something not at all common in our classrooms today.

Vivien: It may be awkward to slow our pace, but if we think of the impact we can have by helping students identify the deeper assumptions, values, and beliefs underpinning their behaviors (and our society)—we are creating a powerful awareness, which is the first prerequisite for change.

Julia: Indeed, because more than a singular reflection, we are developing the habit of critically reflecting—and yes, we all have to slow down for that.

Nick: This is not new—it has been at the core of ancient wisdom and modern scholarly research, so perhaps we have just allowed ourselves to be distracted by our over-burdened lifestyle. Time to pause. Let's reflect on that. ☺

CHAPTER 9

Principle 4: Self-Awareness

Know thyself.

—Inscription in the forecourt of the
Temple of Apollos at Delphi

Definition

Building self-awareness in people through helping them understand
the relation between what they feel, think, and act, and their impact on
others, is a crucial step toward their greater personal and professional
competence.

*Julia: I see this as a learning outcome, rather than a learning principle. Why
is it listed as a principle?*

You have a good point. We can see self-awareness as a goal, and many
learning situations aim at it, that is, therapy sessions, self-help groups,
coaching relationships, and self-development programs. The reason it is
raised to the level of a learning principle is based on the extreme importance and the role that self-awareness plays in our life. We have a great
need to understand ourselves, and we spontaneously seek to do so; it is
built into our nature. We also want to understand others, and this in turn
leads us to understand ourselves too, how we feel, react, and why. Perhaps
it is a principle as well as a goal. Consider this: Is there any learning
situation that you can imagine that is not linked to understanding ourselves, whether it is the role we play in the learning process or the feelings
we experience as a result? We are even involved in the ethical implications when we apply things we learn, for example, financial instruments
or marketing strategies. So can you fathom any knowledge outside the

person, any intellectual event that happens independently of the learner and his life?

Vivien: Well, I can think of many—if not most—of the classes I have taken in my life that were taught as intellectual events: They were objective, factual, independent of who I am, and what was going on in my life at that time, or how I felt or would use the information ....

No doubt. The principles we are discussing are certainly not mainstream learning approaches. But let me ask you, how effective would you say your learning experiences have been, when, as you describe them, they appealed solely to your intellect and ignored the rest of you?

Vivien: I think they were effective, and it was comfortable that I didn't have to make many connections, or "linking" as you say, to what the lesson meant. I didn't have to engage myself deeply, I just had to learn, and mainly, simply memorize. Now that I think of it, it was also a way to compartmentalize myself .... What I learned was ultimately disconnected from my life, and didn't have much relevance to it. Actually there were some exceptions, which I realize happened with teachers or teaching moments when we had a different type of conversation; moments when we ... talked about what meaning it had for us. ... I think I understand what you mean.

That is the point. The fact that our institutional education is focusing on concepts and data assumed to exist independently of our life makes it sound objective and scientific. Yet, as we apply what we learned, we have to connect it to our life, use it in our work, in our context—and on ourselves. For this reason, making self-awareness a structural component of every learning situation helps anchor the contents in a more profound way.

Andres: I guess it also engages the learner more.

Yes, and we have to keep in mind that the ultimate purpose of learning is that students may become responsible leaders, so self-awareness is both engaging and vital.

Nick: Self-awareness is addressed in behavioral sciences, yet it becomes a learning principle here?

How is learning not a behavior? I think we fall into the trap of fragmenting ideas, concepts, and contents. We say, "It is either behavioral science, or a learning theory." Let's go back in time. We all have heard about the aphorism sculpted at the entrance to the Greek temple of Apollo in the city of Delphi: "Know thyself." John Locke[1] wrote about identity and diversity in *An Essay Concerning Human Understanding* in 1689, and this is considered one of the first elaborations on consciousness, a concept linked to self-awareness. For Locke, consciousness means recognizing oneself. According to Locke, personal identity (the self) depends on consciousness.* Was this early behavioral science or philosophy?

Self-awareness has been the focus of much scholarly writing. The early behavioral scientist William James[2] described the role of introspection in increasing self-awareness. Sigmund Freud,[3] and authors influenced by his theories (Anna Freud, Carl F. Jung, William Reich, Alfred Adler, Melanie Klein, David Winnicott, Jacques Lacan, to name a few), extensively researched the importance of feelings and thoughts and their link to the unconscious reasons of our behaviors. Throughout behavioral sciences we find the shared belief that we develop as human beings as we increase our consciousness (Kegan,[4] Torbert,[5] Wilber[6]). Further, in humanistic psychology, self-awareness is seen as a way to expand our understanding of ourselves and to improve our relationships with others in the world (Rogers[7]).

Many studies focused on developing instruments to increase self-awareness, and Jung's[8] definition of psychological types became the foundation for Myers and Briggs's[9] instrument to assess behavioral preferences and personality characteristics. The Myers–Briggs Type Indicator (MBTI) is a well-respected psychological instrument used to increase self-awareness, as are the Enneagram, Insights, and the Hogan Assessment.

A further connection between learning and self-awareness was developed by Peter Senge,[10] in his contribution to the field of management

---

* Thanks to Paul Roberts and Boris Drizin for these contributions.

literature *The Fifth Discipline*. Senge lists developing "self-mastery" as one of the five disciplines necessary to build a learning organization. Daniel Goleman,[11] in his book *Emotional Intelligence*, described a type of intelligence different from intellectual intelligence, one involving the ability to understand one's own and others' emotions. In this perspective, self-awareness plays a key role in personal competence and self-management. More recent studies[12] see emotional intelligence (understanding the self) as an important means to develop a sustainability mindset.

In the field of education, Jack Mezirow[13] elaborated on the importance of uncovering one's own assumptions to increase self-awareness, which, he argues, creates transformational learning. Many other educational scholars (Freire,[14] Argyis,[15] Schon,[16] Brookfield,[17] Cranton,[18] Kegan[19]) have referred to the importance of uncovering assumptions to increase self-awareness and awareness of the social, political, and cultural environment to which the self is connected. They all see the intimate linkage between understanding self, consciousness, and change.

Vivien: Is this the reason that self-awareness is a principle to help us develop responsible managers?

Definitely. If we want to change how the new generation acts in the world, we need to embed prompts to help them become aware of their own beliefs, values, assumptions, preferences, and habits. The first step of transformation is self-awareness, then we can revisit and review if we want to change anything, if we will be meeting our goals or living up to our values if we don't change our own perspectives or habits. Recent studies point to a shift in the conception of humans, from *Homo economicus*—an individualistic, self-interested, and rational economic man—to the *Homo sustinens*,[20] where the social dimension of human existence is considered as well as emotional and evolutionary aspects. In this conception, moral responsibility is seen as an important determinant of human action due to humans' history as a "being in community." Contemporary philosopher Ken Wilber even designed a program to develop the Integral Operating System (IOS), which aims at helping participants reach higher levels of consciousness, move from temporary states of awareness to more permanent stages of consciousness, and this includes seeing ourselves as part of a larger societal—planetary or even cosmic whole.[21]

Andres: What are some ways to include this principle into our classes?

There are many possibilities, starting with questions to use in a guided reflection exercise, questions that allow the students to make meaning out of readings or data that we present. For example: What does this mean for me, for my life, my values, and my habits? We can use this process having a dialogue, journaling, in individual silent reflection, or by writing assignments. Providing feedback to the students, preferably in one-on-one conversations, is also a valuable way to contribute to self-awareness. However, this requires the acceptance of the student to receive the feedback. Unsolicited feedback (even if constructive) can be difficult to process, and the suggestion is that the educator makes an offer and provides the feedback only when requested.

Other ways to enact this principle are through instruments that help students identify their learning styles or preferences, like the Learning Styles Inventory,[22] or as mentioned before, the MBTI questionnaire, that defines people as belonging to one of 16 personality types. Our personality type marks our tendency or preference to manage, learn, lead, relate to others, think, perceive, and decide in different ways. Since developing responsible managers is intimately connected with changing how we act, these instruments can be valuable tools. They help us understand our own individual perspective of the world as one of many possible perspectives, and not necessarily the best or most privileged position.

Andres: I have difficulties imagining how in a course teaching technical content we could incorporate self-assessment instruments, something so personal.

Well, perhaps an accounting class is not the appropriate one in which to introduce such an instrument, but you could always use questions that help students explore, for example, what their preferred learning style is, and consider those styles when planning your classes and assignments. However, in other courses that are preparing students for leadership roles, self-assessment instruments can be of great value, and in fact are a critical component in corporate leadership development programs. I'd like to make a note. In order for the learning to become "personal," as you say, to become more than an intellectual exchange of data, it is important first to create a safe environment, where students are appreciated, where feelings are treated with respect, and where judgment is suspended both by us as instructors and by the students.

> *Nick: Summarizing, this is another ancient concept—back to the Greeks or probably even further back. It is present in philosophy, behavioral sciences, personal development approaches, human development theories, and even learning theories. And critically exploring our assumptions and values allows us to not only understand ourselves, but is also at the foundation of social change.*
>
> *Andres: We can bring this principle to life by prompts to stimulate thinking about our values and identity, also by using learning or personality styles instruments, and even making offers to provide one-on-one feedback. But most importantly, we need first to create a respectful, appreciative, nonjudging setting.*
>
> *Julia: Self-awareness is both content and a learning principle to help us understand ourselves, where we are coming from, and also how we could impact the world. It is independent of what discipline we are teaching or working on, because when knowledge has to be put into action, humans are the agents behind the action.*
>
> *Vivien: And by understanding ourselves, we can be more accepting of others, and of diversity, something very important if we want to bring about change: change makers are never mainstream, so we need to help our students to be prepared to encounter resistance and delays, to develop resilience, and not to take rejection personally. By gaining self-awareness they will become wiser, more conscious, perhaps more effective leaders, and more powerful change agents.*

CHAPTER 10

Principle 5: Social Learning

Learn from the mistakes of others. You can never live long enough to make them all yourself.

—Groucho Marx

Definition

Learning emerges through social interaction and, therefore, individuals multiply their learning opportunities.

Julia: I can see that clearly, and actually it seems pretty obvious since we are talking about classrooms where students get together to learn. Why is this singled out as a principle?

It depends on what classroom you have in mind. If it is a typical classroom, with rows of tables, or an amphitheater, chances are that the most interaction the students will have will be as they get into or out of their seats!

The setting plays a major role in allowing for interaction, although of course it is not sufficient. Some classrooms have modern and functional tables that can be regrouped and moved around, but this alone does not guarantee social learning if the instructor's sole teaching style is to stand in front of the class and lecture and if he ignores the benefits that movable furniture can provide. Many courses are set up for a one-to-many relationship, with the expert addressing the audience, and, occasionally, with some of the audience asking or replying to a question. Many instructors intuitively use this principle when they sense the energy level in the room is decreasing, and they quickly ask the students to have a discussion or share their thoughts with their neighbors, in trios or small groups. This technique changes the atmosphere and boosts the energy as everyone becomes engaged. When we think of this as a principle, it helps us to remember the importance of learning with and from one another, not only as a way of engaging the audience.

Andres: Other than sharing learning with a neighbor, what other techniques do you suggest to bring this principle to life?

Debriefs are easy ways to generate learning between one another. After a video, an activity, a project, or a presentation, we can dedicate 5 minutes to a debrief, based on simple questions, such as asking "What did you learn about this topic?" and "What strikes you as important about what we have just heard?" In this way, we foster making the learning conscious, and students have an opportunity to link it to their own reality, and also to hear different takeaways from their colleagues. This practice of taking a few minutes to debrief segments of the session can be made into an integral, and powerful, part of the learning process.

Dialogues are another way to promote social learning. A dialogue is different from a discussion: The focus is on listening to each other, suspending judgments, building upon what others have said, and collectively weaving meaning out of the skeins of comments heard. Dialogues also require a safe environment, one in which people show respect for others' points of view and appreciation for their sharing of thoughts and feelings. Additionally, I have found it instructive to establish learning partners during a course, creating duos or trios for exchange of learning throughout the program, and periodically sharing their discussions with the larger group. Another simple exercise that can provide great value in terms of social learning is sharing "incidental insights"* after a break—inviting the class to share insights from their break conversations, since sometimes it is then when people share hopes, questions, wishes, or opinions in an informal way.

Vivien: I imagine that social learning is important because it teaches us to accept diversity of perspectives, right?

---

* Thanks to Ernie Turner for this exercise. More exercises can be found in Turner (2013).

That is one of the benefits. Another is that by creating opportunities to listen and share insights, students get to know each other, receiving ideas and inspiration that otherwise they would not have thought of. And since the big challenges we are collectively facing require that we collaborate and develop solutions together, finding ways to promote social learning offers a great arena for training.

A Story

I am known for moving the tables to the sides in every class, and having students sit in a circle of chairs, which is how we have our sessions. At the end of one course, one of the students wrote that one the most valuable aspects of the course was the opportunity to meet his colleagues, to see them eye to eye, to hear their perspectives, to exchange ideas, and to get a glimpse into other people's lives. In all his school years, he only had seen the necks of his colleagues, and as everyone rushes into the classroom and runs out, it never allowed for such a depth of connection with one another. He mentioned how much he had learned from them.

Nick: Is social learning an adult learning principle?

Actually, it is a human learning principle. From the start, we learn from and with others. While the assimilation of learning is personal, a social context always exists to frame and feed the learning. The Soviet psychologist Lev Vygotsky[1] referred to this as "situated learning," indicating that social interaction plays a key role in the development of cognition. He observed that the scope of skills that we develop with guidance or peer collaboration (and competition) exceeds what can be attained alone.

Lave and Wenger[2] call this "relational learning," and noted that classrooms should be set up to promote those connections with one another. When people interact and have an opportunity to share knowledge, skills, history, values, or processes, they create what Wenger calls a "community of practice."[3] Frequently the learning that happens is unintentional, but by designing our courses with social learning in mind, we can convert the *unintentional* impact into an *intentional* resource. Along this line, the Canadian author Albert Bandura[4] states that learning "would be exceedingly laborious, not to mention hazardous, if people had to rely solely on the effects of their own actions to inform them what to do. Fortunately, most human behavior is learned observationally through modeling."

Vivien: Do you mean that our students model behavior to one another?

Yes, they inspire each other to see what is possible, and we as instructors do so too. If we aim at developing change leaders, we can emphasize to our students how they will be themselves modeling behaviors, which others then may adopt. We can do this unintentionally, or with conscious intention, which is more powerful.

> *Vivien: Summarizing, if we embed opportunities of learning from each other we will help students experience it and extrapolate how they could themselves inspire others outside of the classroom, particularly if they model responsible leadership behaviors.*
>
> *Andres: True, and we can add other techniques to the traditional information sharing, such as creating Learning Partners for a more regular sharing, or making it a habit to leave a few minutes for periodic debriefs, so all can reflect on what they have learned.*
>
> *Nick: If we are aware of the potential of creating a learning community in the classroom, of maximizing the opportunities of such a "situated learning," the students may feel they are more than a group of individuals, but perhaps a real team of pioneers.*
>
> *Julia: Yes, and it takes a conscious decision from our side as instructors to make space for sharing and exchange of learning. I believe it challenges the traditional assumption that we owe the students just our knowledge and expertise, and that is what we are there to do. These practices make it clear that there is more potential in the room than what we have to provide.*

CHAPTER 11

Principle 6: Paradigm Shift

If you change the way you look at things, the things you look at change.
—Wayne Dyer

Definition

The most significant learning occurs when individuals are able to shift the perspective by which they habitually view the world, leading to greater understanding both of the world and of others.

Nick: Is this related to the concept of paradigm that Kuhn described?

Yes, Kuhn[1] defines paradigm as that which "stands for the entire constellation of beliefs, values and techniques, shared by the members of a community." Paradigms shape how we perceive the world and are reinforced by those around us. They condition our interpretations of reality and our worldview. Kuhn's theory represented an important conceptual shift from the positivist scientific model, where a reality was assumed to exist "out there," and which we could get to know through our senses. The positivist view of the world is anchored on a true–false, right–wrong polarity, and science is the only valid way to get at the truth, to understand the world, and to make valid predictions explaining causal relations between variables. Science from a positivist framework is mechanistic.

In contrast, the new approach was called "constructivist," suggesting that we construct reality as we see it through a number of mostly unconscious filters, such as language, age, gender, personal history, education, personal preferences, and development stage. All of these shape our mental maps. There is not one truth, but many, and they can all be integrated, as when we look at an object from different angles.

Julia: Why does this matter for learning?

For example, let's imagine we see the world in terms of an objective reality out there, and we get to know it through our senses (also "common sense"). We see the world in terms of "right" or "wrong." In that sense, authority—based on expertise, age, or mastery—defines who has it right. This is characteristic of the domination model we discussed before. As we evolve our thinking, this model is slowly becoming outdated. We can observe it in any debate: There are many ways to interpret data.

Nick: This reminds me of the stages of human development, as elaborated by scholars such as Robert Kegan,[2] Bill Torbert,[3] Ken Wilber,[4] who see more integrated ways of relating to the world—from "it's all about me and I'm right" (or wrong) to more inclusive and integrative perspectives.

Absolutely, so it is an opportunity for us as educators to challenge our students' certainties, and perhaps trigger new ways of thinking and acting in the world.

Julia: Is this principle based on the assumption that currently we are not developing "responsible managers," and that to get there, we need to shift our or their values?

That is a bit too strong; but we can say that not enough business schools around the world are aware of their responsibility—and their opportunity—to develop young leaders who can actively shape a better world.

Of course, no one is intentionally developing *irresponsible* leaders, but when we take a look into the contents and methods that represent the essence of advanced education, we find entrenched traditional top-down lecturing that serves to further the domination model. In the way programs are organized into subjects, we also find "siloed" contents that foster a fragmented vision of reality and obscure the interconnections; rather short-term thinking; consideration of nature as a resource rather than humans being a part of nature; and rare inclusion of all stakeholders into the picture—including the next seven generations. This may sound strange, but it is old wisdom from the Iroquois Nation's Law of Peace that in every decision, be it personal, governmental, or corporate, we must consider how it will affect our descendants seven generations into the future.

Nick: Your list suggests curriculum content, and we were discussing "paradigm shift" as a principle. I am confused ....

Method and outcome, at times it is difficult to distinguish between them, just as when we talk about sustainability or responsibility: Are they means or ends? They are both. In this case, I was illustrating with some examples how we may—unintentionally—be developing managers who are not properly prepared for the task awaiting them. The core of this principle is to find ways to uncover and identify the mental models and maps we carry in our mind, so that we can become aware of them, and eventually choose to keep or modify them.

Alford Korzybski,[5] the father of general semantics—the branch of linguistics and logic concerned with meaning—indicated in 1933 that "the map is not the territory," pointing to the fact that our perception of reality is not reality itself but our own version of it, or our "map." Unless we take notice of this, it is difficult to think of real transformative learning. How can we transform our behaviors if we are unaware of the mental models and maps that shape or condition our decisions and habits?

Nick: Is this more a philosophical concept than a learning theory?

A number of educators (Cranton,[6] Mezirow,[7] Brookfield[8]) and also management scholars such as Argyris,[9] Schön,[10] and Senge[11] observe that learning needs to incorporate critical thinking and to promote self-reflection, and instructors should have the aim of uncovering one's mental models and assumptions, which are mostly unconscious, so that they can be examined. Some educators came to this understanding by the ways of social action theory (such as Freire[12] and Horton et al.[13]) or feminism (Belenky et al.[14] Gilligan[15]), all highlighting the importance of unconscious mental models in shaping our actions. They see the main purpose of learning is to become critical thinkers, and the educators' role is to help uncover and surface these mental models and assumptions. Our decisions and actions are based on our interpretation of the world, and if that interpretation changes, so will our actions. There is an agreement among educators that the ultimate goal of education is to lead to more informed, conscious actions.

Andres: How could we implement this principle in a course?

There are many activities that can be used to implement this principle. A powerful one is to ask students to list their assumptions about a particular issue.

A Story

On one occasion, I asked the group to write down their assumptions around work–life balance. When they reported what they had written, they noticed that they all thought that work was the more important of the two, because income depended on it, but personal time, while important, was not possible or realistic. Because the group agreed in this perspective, they indicated that it was not simply an assumption, but a reality. Does the mere fact that a group shares the same assumption make it a reality? Considering something "a reality" gives us the feeling that it is something we have to accept and that we cannot change. On the other hand, looking at it as an assumption is empowering, because it implies that we have some control of our life, and opens up the possibility that we can choose an option and modify it to our benefit.

Another way to bring the principle of Paradigm Shift to life is to place the students in unfamiliar situations. This can be done by having them engage with people outside of their normal circle. For instance, you can suggest that they interview a homeless person; someone belonging to another race, or ethnic group; a religious fundamentalist; or someone belonging to a different age group, profession, or nationality. This exercise triggers them to see the world through other eyes, and trains them in recognizing other people's mental maps. This invariably has an impact on their personal assumptions, since they realize that what they take for granted is actually just another interpretation of the world.

Vivien: How does this lead to responsible management?

Until we learn that we act out of our mental maps, we all are fundamentalists, thinking there is one way—the right way. Responsible management however requires that we integrate multiple perspectives, that we listen to different stakeholders as we analyze a problem or make a decision. As the American adult educator Jack Mezirow[16] indicates, it is easier to see how others are different from us than to become aware of our own assumptions and how we understand our society. As educators, we have an opportunity to use certain activities as a mirror held up in front of our students (and ourselves, of course!).

Andres: Can you give us an example of how to incorporate such an "unfamiliar" environment in the design of a course?

The activities can happen inside or outside the classroom. Students can be grouped into project teams with lots of differences—gender, age, religion, culture, language preference, areas of interest. They quickly discover their own paradigms and begin to see other points of view. Outside the classroom, a trip, a visit to a neighborhood that is not part of the students' life are some other options.

Two Stories

Soraia Schuttel is a professor at Unisinos, a large university in Porto Alegre, Brazil, where she teaches a management class. She took her students to a residence for youths from poor, disadvantaged families, some of them orphans, or with parents in jail, and tasked her students with designing a financial education class for the children.

Amelia Naim, teaching at IPMI, a business school in Jakarta, Indonesia, encouraged her students to work with families in a very low-income district. This was, for the students, the first time they had interacted with poverty. First they participated in sweeping the dirt floor of the house; they then all sat on that floor where they had illuminating conversations about the challenges faced by the families. One result of the talk was that the students made and helped execute a plan that helped the families create a vegetable garden to provide for their own food. After that experience, several of the students reflected on how this activity had influenced their thoughts on their own future work. For example, some, who were planning to work in their large family business after graduation, stated their determination to influence their family company into considering low-income populations when making their business plans.

> Julia: *This principle, in summary, emphasizes that learning, in essence, is the process of surfacing and critically scrutinizing the mental models that we have created to make sense of how we view, and act in, the world. An important, and at times profound, possible outcome of learning can be development of a different mental model or perspective from which to view the world.*
>
> Nick: *This is actually indicated by learning scholars to be the core purpose of teaching and learning: that students become more aware, and act in more informed ways.*
>
> Vivien: *Yes, but not "any" informed ways. As we develop leaders, we must attempt to ensure that students become more responsible leaders who are intent on shaping a better world.*
>
> Andres: *We can embed into our course projects that take students out of the classroom, into the "real world," to unfamiliar contexts, because that will present the best opportunities for seeing the world through other eyes, and for identifying their own mental maps. But even without going out of the classroom we can ask challenging questions, ask to notice our assumptions or practice to speak from within some stranger's perspective.*

CHAPTER 12

Principle 7: Systems Thinking

Each life reverberates in every other life. Whether or not we acknowledge it, we are connected, woven together in our needs and desires, rich and poor, men and women alike.

—Susan Griffin

Definition

We live in a complex, interconnected, cocreated world, and, in order to better understand and tackle individual and organizational issues, we have to take into account the different systems and contexts that mutually influence one another.

Julia: It's clear why this is important: because too much in our education is presented in a fragmented fashion, as if subjects existed in isolation. But every issue is interconnected with many other factors. I think this also relates to expanding our own thinking, to training our students to see beyond our right–wrong duality, as we discussed earlier, and to helping them look for interrelations in everything. Is that what you mean?

Yes, although we always are only *partially* right since we cannot comprehend the full extension of all the possibilities. But it is an important step to install in the "operating system" of the mind—the understanding that everything is interconnected.

Vivien: An important step toward more responsible management?

Yes, because when we automatically analyze situations seeking what may be the systemic interconnections, we are actively looking for other stakeholders involved in the issue, and gauging how they might see it. Imagine for a moment if all business decisions were made only after weighing how all the stakeholders might be impacted, including nature and our future generations. What do you think this would lead to?

*Vivien: I think, for a start, we would all be actively creating a more sustainable planet .... (Would we ever be able to consider **all** stakeholders!?)*

Nick: Perhaps not, but it is worth the try. And wouldn't that be an appropriate and timely purpose of education! Yet the theory of systems is not new ....

True. It was Austrian biologist Ludwig von Bertalanffy[1] who first proposed the concept of systems thinking in the 1940s. Not surprisingly the theory originates in biology, a domain that clearly shows the complex interconnections in nature. As a reaction to the reductionist approach in science of that time, von Bertalanffy observed that all elements of any living system were connected, creating webs of relationships. The whole had different properties than the isolated components, and the components influenced both each other and the whole. Systems thinking is a way of focusing on wholes rather than parts, and considers relationships and processes rather than separate entities.[2]

As it frequently happens, at around the same time, the concept of interconnected parts was a topic of study and discussion in the field of cybernetics. Cybernetics was defined by Norbert Wiener in 1948 as "the scientific study of control and communication in the animal and the machine."[3] Elements are seen as relating to each other through transfer of information and "feedback." The field of cybernetics was a joint development of a diverse group of researchers—American applied mathematician Norbert Wiener, British psychiatrist William Ross Ashby,[4] Hungarian mathematician John von Neumann, and Austrian physicist and philosopher Heinz von Foerster—who worked on it in the 1940s and 1950s. Margaret Mead, the American anthropologist and her husband, Gregory Bateson, also participated in these meetings, and significantly contributed to the development of the field. Systems theory has since been applied to multiple domains: family therapy and general psychotherapy,[5] neuro-linguistic programming,[6] social sciences;[7] political science and social action;[8] business, management and organizational theory;[9] economics;[10] ecology;[11] engineering; developmental psychology;[12] sustainability;[13] and more recently also in education for sustainability.[14]

A Story

Ashish Pandey is a professor at the Indian Institute of Technology in Mumbai. He teaches management, and has one central learning goal for his whole course: That the students understand and assimilate the concept of interconnectedness, so that it becomes part of their lens to view, and act in, the world. He explained that it is a very ancient teaching present in the Vedanta tradition.

For our conversation, the history of systems thinking within the behavioral sciences is of particular interest. It underlies the model of the Gestalt Psychology of Wolfgang Köhler[15], and German research-ers Max Wertheimer[16] and Kurt Koffka[17] applied Gestalt theory to problem-solving, noting that the separate parts of a problem should not be studied in isolation, but should be seen as a whole. Kurt Lewin[18] developed his "Field Theory" based on Gestalt principles, indicating that behaviors were determined by the totality of an individual's context, as opposed to a single cause-and-effect relationship. In field theory, a "field" is defined as the totality of coexisting facts that are conceived of as mutually interdependent.

Organizational learning author Peter Senge introduced the concept of systems thinking as one of the five basic disciplines that would allow an organization to learn. He suggested that in order to survive in an increasingly complex world, we had to expand our thinking and include different perspectives, going beyond the immediate stimulus–response connections, and consider the larger picture of interconnections and long-term impact of our decisions.

Nick: Indigenous cultures also celebrate the interconnections with Nature through rituals.

Definitively, and interconnectedness has been an ancient teaching present in all the major religions of our civilization: Buddhism, in the sacred texts of Hinduism, in the Quran, Judaism, and Christianity.

Andres: Can you give us some ideas on how to bring this principle into the classroom?

One simple way has been mentioned before—linking what the students are experiencing or learning with other contexts, outside the immediate "here and now," so that they expand their perspectives and understandings, and discover new relations and interconnections. For those students with a preference for visual learning, you can form small groups and invite them to create a graphic representation of the different components or factors connected to the topic of study. This can create interesting visual webs of interrelationships, and images can reinforce the message.

Another way to emphasize the scope and impact of systems theory is to ask the class to list all the stakeholders in a decision or action that they, students, take during any day. Two simple questions can suffice. Who were the individuals involved in making your coffee-drinking experience possible today? Who and what is impacted by you drinking your coffee?

Additionally, conducting a dialogue about the implications of including stakeholders' perspectives in a decision—or selecting which ones to consider—is another means to help people to develop the habit of adopting a systems view.

> *Julia: Summarizing, the systems perspective is an antidote to our fragmented understanding of reality. And while fragmenting makes us feel we can master a complex challenge, it is an illusion because everything, everywhere is interconnected. We need to correct that myopia with some systemic spectacles.*
>
> *Vivien: It seems to me that we won't be able to tackle and solve the big problems of our society and planet if we approach them with the usual one-sided perspective. We need to understand how we are all interrelated,*

and the impact our decisions and actions can have on the future and across the globe. The bad and the good decisions too. Or should I say, the bad and the good impacts of any decision. As educators, we of course cannot ensure perfection, but we can at least strive toward facilitating a responsible management education.

Nick: *The timing is right, urgent in fact, although the importance of considering the web of connections has been identified almost a century ago. Actually, interconnectedness has been present in ancient sacred texts, not to mention in so many indigenous rituals.*

Andres: *We don't need any training to introduce this principle into our classes, just remember to ask: Who are the stakeholders involved? What patterns do you see? What will this decision mean, in the perspective of time, to future generations? We can talk about it, make graphs, or dramatizations, anything that can install a new lens into the students' minds.*

CHAPTER 13

Principle 8: Integration

If a man is to live, he must be all alive, body, soul, mind, heart, spirit.
—Thomas Merton

Definition

People are a combination of mind, body, soul, and emotions, and respond best when all aspects of their being are considered, engaged, and valued.

Julia: I must say this sounds like a theme for a retreat rather than a classroom, where the key point is to engage the intellect!

That is a fair observation: Retreats pay attention to those different dimensions of the participants so as to provide a holistic experience. They are, in general, deeply satisfying events from which people emerge with renewed energy, deeper insights, or new goals. If you have participated in such an event, you can probably evoke the feeling just by remembering the retreat.

On the other hand, I suspect it might be difficult to recall a strictly intellectual, cognitive learning event that left you with the same feelings of engagement and satisfaction. It may even be difficult to recall what exactly you learned in the many hours of lectures—and when we are seeking transformational learning, it is not enough to address the intellect. The totality of an individual's potential is in play; the whole person needs to be engaged.

Vivien: I think that the importance of integrating all these other nonintellectual dimensions support, and are indeed part of, our specific purpose, which is to develop responsible leaders intent on assessing the scope of their role in the world. Since students normally don't ponder their role in the world, we need to aim at providing transformational learning experiences that engage the whole person.

That is a good reason. And this brings us back to a point we discussed earlier: Is there any profession or activity that would benefit from ignoring the desirability—and consequence—of achieving "responsible planetary citizenship?" If we are all seeking a better world, wouldn't it be natural for everyone to operate from within such a framework? Which means that *any educational content* should have the aim of expanding awareness, of achieving more informed and conscious actions.

Looking at this too from the different perspective of the learner: Have you ever been in an intense lecture or session that demanded all your intellectual focus, and have the instructor suddenly tell a joke, making the whole audience laugh out loud, releasing tensions and bringing refreshing energy into the room? We are multidimensional beings. To artificially fragment us by leaving out our physical needs of movement and stretching, our emotions that color our life, our spiritual needs that bring a deeper dimension to our days, how can that be good for learning!?

Andres: In other words, you are suggesting that we should bring humor into the class as a way to implement this principle?

Humor is good; it creates a more relaxed atmosphere. A very creative use of fun was used by Rita Shea-Van Fossen, a professor of Organizational Behaviour at Nova Southeastern University, who brought a dead fish into her first class. She tossed it in the fashion the fish mongers in a famous Seattle fish market do it, to make the point of four characteristics:

Play—having fun since we spend most of our waking hours at work
Be there—Being present to each other (and our customers and our
    work)
Make their day—Doing things to help each other out—going out of
    your way to help others and
Choose your attitude—Choosing the right attitude when you come
    to work (class)

These characteristics referred to how the market operates, but they serve as inspiration on how to create a positive working atmosphere that also engages clients. The powerful experience creates a lasting learning for the students.

And there are multiple other ways to address the whole person in the classroom. They don't have to be related to learning or to schoolwork. For example, you can start the session with a "check in," asking what was the "best of the day"—a memorable event—and hearing from everyone (or if the group is large, having them share with their neighbor). I like to start my classes with a minute of guided meditation, a practice that is rather unfamiliar for most of the students. I invite them to close their eyes, which helps them go inside themselves and be less self-conscious about participating in a very unusual exercise in the classroom, to feel their body on the chair, their feet on the floor. I may ask them to pay attention to their breath, nothing else. This simple activity creates a whole new atmosphere, particularly since everyone is living in such a fast pace.

Andres: I cannot quite see myself doing a guided meditation, it feels a bit awkward, and besides, wouldn't the students feel uncomfortable and reject it?

Certainly, first we need to feel comfortable with the idea ourselves, as with everything. Doing a practice on our own, guided by a meditation on You Tube, is an accessible way to try it out and learn how to guide the one-minute exercise.

But there is another aspect that you are pointing out, which is key: the importance of creating a safe environment. This cannot be sufficiently stressed. If we want to promote a holistic, meaningful learning experience, we need to ensure that the students feel safe, respected, appreciated, and that they can trust the instructor to maintain those conditions in the room. It is also important that we explain what we are inviting them to do, why, how it will work, and what they can get out of it: This framing helps to develop trust, relaxes everyone by addressing the different learning styles in the room, and sets the classroom up for a good learning session.

Communication channels need to stay open, so that students are comfortable when invited to provide feedback, and so that they speak up if something is not working for them. This brings me to another important step: to set clear norms and agreements on what the mutual expectations will be. It is not just the instructor who sets the expectation; she also needs to invite the students to express theirs (as we saw when exploring the Principle Relevance) in order to create ownership of the learning.

Andres: These recommendations seem to be less related to the principle but to creating a positive working atmosphere.

Actually they are connected. It would not be possible to invite expression of feelings, concerns, hopes, expectations, or to close eyes in a meditation, or give candid feedback if the individuals didn't feel safe and trusting. And we as instructors also have to allow ourselves to show up with more than our intellect.

Andres: You have given some examples of how to implement this principle by addressing one's body (to calm down, relax), and one's soul (the minute of meditation). Can you give some ideas for engaging feelings?

As we saw in the first part of this book, the role of the instructor has to evolve to accompany the changing characteristics of the audience, and become more of a curator, someone who can help to make meaning out of data. Asking the students how the contents relate to their life, values, and how they feel about certain themes is a way to address them from a holistic perspective. Other ways of addressing the whole person are activities that engage the different intelligences, for example, the intuitive knowledge, the emotional, musical, artistic, or spiritual intelligence when the topic permits it. When teaching hard sciences, invite them to change seats, to stretch, to discuss things standing up; when teaching social sciences, invite them to express ideas in drawings, relationships through metaphors and analogies, feelings through colors, images, or poetry.

A Story

Students of Professor Amelia Naim, who teaches in a business school in Jakarta, Indonesia, were preparing their presentations and one team talked about the importance of managing stress and of taking care of one's health to be a more balanced and effective leader. They suggested that to achieve this, the leaders must lead a life of less sedentary days and more movement. Then, to underscore the message out, they played a YouTube video of a famous pop star and invited the whole class to get up and dance following the steps on the screen. Right in the classroom!

It's probably safe to say that they thought this class was anything but boring. The student-led activity made them understand how a rational suggestion (to take care of our health and review our lifestyle) was something that connected to their real life, to their dreams of the future, to their whole person. And it was the teacher who had created a climate where this was possible.

Nick: Is this principle based on Gardiner's theory of multiple intelligences?

Yes, and the notion of integration or holistic learning is rooted in humanistic psychology. This theory emerged around the 1950s in North America as a reaction to two schools of thought that were dominating: behaviorism, with an overly experimental research observing animal behavior, emphasis of Pavlov's and Skinner's theories, and the insight-based emphasis of psychoanalysis. These schools of thought didn't focus on values, and Abraham Maslow and Clark Moustakas started forums for colleagues who were interested in considering a more humanistic vision. They started a new movement discussing being, meaning, self-actualization, health, creativity, and development, which they considered essential for their new approach to psychology. This led to the foundation of the American Association for Humanistic Psychology with members such as Gordon Allport, Charlotte Buhler, Abraham Maslow (transpersonal psychology), Rollo May, and Carl Rogers (person-based counseling), Fritz Perls (Gestalt psychology), and Wilhelm Reich (body-based psychotherapies). This movement aimed at a fuller concept of what it means to be human. But it was not totally new: It brought back perspectives expressed long ago by other civilizations, like the Hebrews, the Greeks, and the European Renaissance.

Humanistic psychology suggests that all learning is emotionally grounded, and that our mental models are not just cognitive constructs, but also attached to deep levels of identity and feelings. This means that when we learn, we need to allow for a connection between the intellect and the emotions, something Daniel Goleman[1] has developed in the concept of emotional intelligence, and which acknowledges the importance of emotions in our thoughts and actions.

Building on this, other scholars integrated spiritual and cultural perspectives to better understand the human experience. Ken Wilber, whom we mentioned before, has developed an integral theory of consciousness, which draws on disciplines such as psychology, sociology, philosophy, mysticism, postmodernism, empirical science, ecology, Buddhism, and systems theory. Elizabeth Tisdell[2] and an increasing number of scholars incorporate secular spirituality into the learning process to allow participants a full expression of themselves. The purpose of education feeds into this expansion of consciousness and promotes the consideration of the body, mind, emotions, and soul to develop more aware, free, and responsible individuals.

> *Vivien: Summarizing, the challenge to develop responsible citizens of the world calls for finding ways to engage our students in the most holistic way—not only their minds, but also what shapes their thoughts and actions, namely, their feelings, values, physicality, and their soul. That will create powerful, proactive change agents who act with a vision and the passion to take it to fruition.*
>
> *Nick: We need to revisit more ancient wisdom about living in sync with ourselves, with Nature, and with each other. History is replete with a number of scholars who sought to integrate many disciplines into understanding human nature: philosophy, sociology, ecology, psychology, spirituality, neuro-psychology, systems thinking, mysticism, and hard sciences. Learning and human development align in educating for conscious and informed actions.*
>
> *Andres: The diversity of dimensions (mind, body, feelings, and soul) demand that instructors consider new creative techniques: stretching, meditation, walking meetings, relaxation, dancing, creative writing, artistic expression, humor, walks in Nature, and more. For this to happen, it is*

essential for educators to create a safe and trusting environment; equally importantly, the instructors must also take a risk, perhaps move out of their comfort zone, so that they, too, can feel the liberation—and the power—of expressing themselves in a holistic way.

Julia: *The reason this principle of Integration is so important is that we are increasingly living fragmented lives that create stress and health problems. We become disconnected from our self and from each other. As teachers we can lead a change, remembering that we don't teach accounting, physics, marketing, or leadership: We are helping students learn.*

CHAPTER 14

Principle 9: Repetition and Reinforcement

One looks back with appreciation to the brilliant teachers, but with gratitude to those who touched our human feelings. The curriculum is so much necessary raw material, but warmth is the vital element for the growing plant and for the soul of the child.

—Carl Jung

Definition

Practice brings mastery and positive reinforcement increases the assimilation.

Nick: This sounds very different from all the principles we have been discussing. They were humanistic, cognitivist, or based on a postmodern constructivist paradigm, and this sounds like old classic behaviorism: linear cause–effect.

That is true! And it is one of the interesting characteristics of Action Reflection Learning (ARL). Remember that this learning methodology emerged thanks to the intellectual freedom of the practitioners who developed it, who didn't allow themselves to be limited by conceptual frameworks. They simply used what seemed to work in order to create powerful learning experiences and transformative learning, which is the deepest and most evolutionary type of learning that exists.

Behaviorism (Watson,[1] Skinner,[2] Pavlov) dominated American psychology from about 1900 to 1970. It was based on empirically observable behaviors, as opposed to subjective phenomena such as consciousness, feelings, or personal meaning given to situations. You can recognize in it the traditional classroom pedagogy, which was founded on this framework.

Learning was seen as dependent on conditions of the environment, and the learner was, in Locke's terms, a "tabula rasa." In addition, reinforcements were found to play a key role in learning. Thorndike,[3] for example, described how changes in behavior (i.e., learning) respond to the Law of Effect: "Behavior that is followed by satisfying consequences will be more likely to be repeated and behavior that is followed by unsatisfying consequences will be less likely to be repeated." Watson, one of the first people to obtain a doctorate in psychology in the United States—in 1902—studied the impact of reinforcements. Skinner developed the theory of "operant conditioning," noting that we behave the way we do because a behavior has had certain positive or negative consequences in the past.

Later, the behavioral influence of positive reinforcement led to the study of motivations (Maslow[4]), which further connected not only past experiences as conditioners, but also the future as a motivating possibility. This is seen in scenario planning, in visioning exercises, in goal-setting, and in the use of conscious intention-setting as a draw toward actions. It is the Law of Cause and Effect converted into "the law of cause and promise of effect." To periodically recall our objective (what we informally call the "carrot") becomes a powerful reinforcement, helping us persist in our efforts. External reinforcements were further studied by cognitivists Ausubel[5] and Bandura,[6] who observed that both positive and negative reinforcements have an impact and lead to changes in behavior. The concept of learning by trial and error is also present in experiential learning theory, however, adding to it the importance of the educator who supports active experimentation.[7] ARL incorporates some specific aspects of behaviorist thinking by valuing positive reinforcement, and acknowledges the importance of a supportive attitude on the part of the learning facilitator, who ensures that the learner feels safe in a trusting and accepting environment, who acknowledges and appreciates the learner's achievements, and who offers time and opportunities to try out new behaviors.

The appreciative tone present in this learning approach has roots in Carl Rogers's[8] humanistic therapeutic model, where the therapist offers empathic understanding, appreciation, and a supportive attitude. In the organizational setting, Cooperrider and Whitney[9] applied the humanistic approach in "Appreciative inquiry." Grounded in a constructivist paradigm,[10] this model suggests that if we want to create change and learning in an organization, we need to ask what is working well, because more can be built on strengths than on weaknesses. Appreciative Inquiry uses the successes of individuals and organizations to enhance self-esteem, encourage action, and demonstrate to individuals that they are capable of valuable achievements.

Andres: Can you give us a few examples on how to implement this principle in a classroom?

Appreciation can be shown in many ways. It can be manifest in the feedback provided to students, and particularly in how that feedback is given one on one with the student. This can be useful if the educator considers giving that feedback as she would as a coach would with a paying client, instead of as a traditional teacher exerting her power over the student. Another way is for the teacher to take the time to ask, at the end of a class, what the learners believe has been meaningful or exciting, which can help everyone learn to identify the positive, so it can be intentionally repeated.

Teachers might consider responding to late-comers as they would treat a good friend arriving late, by welcoming them, and assuming that there must be good reasons for the tardiness. Having a follow-up chat to find out what happened, and briefing the student in what he missed are very powerful gestures to create an appreciative atmosphere that brings the best out of everyone. When we think the best of others, we trigger in others an automatic reaction to live up to it.

A Story

In a recent class at the undergraduate level, students were teaming up to work on self-selected projects. I overheard a discussion in one team, where they were looking at the tasks to be distributed, and one member was complaining that she was not able to take on any of those tasks because she had a full-time job, was a single parent, and was attending several other courses at school. Her teammates looked puzzled and frustrated.

I stepped closer and asking for permission to comment, I suggested they build their team based on the strengths they individually had, and not on their shortcomings. By conducting a quick inventory of what skills and possibilities were in the group, they would be better able to find who could do what, and still enjoy being a productive member of the team. They talked a few minutes more and realized that the female member didn't have time to meet or do interviews, but that she had good editing skills and the ability to write up reports in her office.

Another way to develop an appreciative climate is by asking feedback from the students, and explaining that their candid feedback will help you understand better their needs. This may sound very bizarre to many of us, but the reality is that students will state their needs whether we ask for it or not, and they will do it publicly. The free website Rate my Professors is the platform students use to share their frustration and happiness and to describe their experience to other fellow students who may consider taking a class with a certain instructor. In a moderate and descriptive language, students from any institution share what they loved and what didn't work in their instructor's pedagogy—or personal style. (If you have never looked into it, it is a great learning experience for educators that can guide us on what we need to improve.)

Julia: I understand why appreciation creates a positive relationship and an appreciative context that fosters learning, risk-taking in a safe environment, and is more likely to result in reinforcement of learning and of behaviors. What about Repetition, the other "r" in this principle?

In experiential learning, as well as in the classical trial and error, repetition brings mastery. In similar ways, teachers have used this principle for centuries, requesting that students practice, then providing feedback and corrections, and asking them to do it again. Learning is not a one-time event, it is a sequenced process, and educators need to give time to students to transition, learn, and change, independently of the domain.

Vivien: What is the impact of this learning principle of repetition and rein-forcement for our goal of developing responsible managers?

When we talk about developing responsible managers, it is clear by now that we are not referring just to "responsible managers" as any time in history, but specifically in the sense given by United Nations Principles for Responsible Management Education (UN PRME): developing individuals who are able to lead with planet and people in mind, not only profit. We are thus trying to change their habits of mind. Adult educator Jack Mezirow elaborates on the power of repetition in the establishment of what he calls new "habits of mind." The more personal and deeper the learning, the more repetition, challenge combined with educator's support, and time will be needed.

Just don't think of repetition isolated from an appreciative approach, or from the ownership of the learning that we discussed in the principle of "Relevance." I have heard a student complain about a professor who was asking her to rewrite an essay several times, "Just because she wants me to get a better grade! That was her goal, not mine!"

A Story

In a course about the Sustainability Mindset at Fordham University, a graduate student wrote the following reflection:

> I enrolled in this course because I had some questions about sustainability and wanted to learn more. Now that I'm ending the course, I have so many more questions than when I started, that I cannot believe it! But what happened, is that I realized it was not just about learning facts. The most important realization was that I began to scrutinize my own values, my habits, my purpose, and my goals. I guess it's fine that I have many more questions now; that's the purpose.

This comment is a good example of how we can accompany our students' on their journey, and allow them to go at their own pace, particularly when revisiting values or worldviews. It takes repetition in terms of discussing and reflecting on certain topics several times, exploring different angles and emotions. And it takes a positive atmosphere, respectful and appreciative, to allow for such uncertainty to evolve.

Nick: Summarizing, the principle of Repetition and Reinforcement is an interesting example of the statement "nothing more practical than a good theory," because, for the purpose of adult learning, it combines the behaviorist concepts of trial and error, and repetition to gain mastery, with the humanistic appreciative approach, of valuing the best in our students to get the best out of them.

Andres: We can show appreciation in the way we include students, assume the best, respond to them as we would respond to a client we are coaching, help them identify what works, and finally provide—and request—candid feedback. But all this has to be done within a safe, trusting environment, one where we aren't patronizing them or assuming we always know best what they need. And we need to give them time to change, because we are transforming habits of mind and worldviews.

Julia: When we create such a positive climate, we are able to get a positive attitude toward learning, introspection, and risk-taking.

Vivien: And this is what we need in terms of a learning environment when we are aiming at developing more insightful, inquisitive, and creative leaders, who don't see the world challenges as overwhelming realities, but instead see opportunities to act with hope and innovation.

CHAPTER 15

Principle 10: Learning Facilitator

The task of the modern educator is not to cut down jungles, but to irrigate deserts.

—C. S. Lewis

Definition

A specific role exists for an expert in methods and techniques for teaching and learning who can optimize the learning of both individuals and groups.

Julia: Aren't you stating the obvious here, by saying that learning needs a teacher?

I agree it may sound obvious, but then again several of the principles sound obvious too—and they are, however, less commonly considered and abided by than we would expect. Here the nuance is in the how, more than the *who*: This principle points at the fact that when instructors are well prepared with methods and techniques that can create powerful learning, magic can occur.

Nick: Beyond all the suggestions you have been giving about how educators should act, is there a conceptual model in education that explores the instructor, what this principle calls the "learning facilitator"?

Yes, and that is precisely the point. We are calling it a principle because a particular way of conceiving the role of the instructor can make such a difference in the learning process. Within the field of education, a long tradition exists of exploring and discussing the role of an educator. The specific characteristics of the settings, the contents to be taught, and the contexts, including different traditions and cultures, these all matter when it comes to the type of learner–instructor relationship.

As we saw before, directive approaches have been the tradition in hierarchical settings, where the instructor embodies power, expertise, and authority. Even today, it is still easy to find examples around us, because this has been for ages the accepted model, and instructors, teachers, sports coaches, experts, spiritual masters, or gurus, all fall into this category. More recently, we have seen the emergence of more participative approaches in some mentors, advisors, counselors, and personal coaches. And, while positional power is still present, the tone and style of the relationship are more open to exploration and change, and power may be more balanced or shared than in the traditional approach. The expertise may still provide authority, but as author Riane Eisler describes it in her study of educational institutions, when the model is *partnership* rather than domination every individual becomes an active participant, and can blossom.

In educational settings, cognitive psychologists (Piaget[1]), humanistic-oriented theorists (Rogers,[2] Knowles[3]), critical theorists (Freire,[4] Horton et al.,[5] Candy and Brookfield[6]), and learning theorists (Kolb,[7] Mezirow,[8] Schön,[9] Cranton[10]) emphasize different aspects of the role of the teacher or facilitator, but *all* acknowledge the importance of some type of support to maximize the learning experience.

Andres: Is the key message then about how we should act, meaning that we should play more of a "learning facilitator" role?

We are seeing an evolution from more top-down, hierarchical, domination models in society to more participative forms of relationship, where individuals retrieve basic rights to express themselves, to choose for themselves, to listen to their passion and interests rather than to their obligations; where individuals are driven by intrinsic motivations more than extrinsic ones. In a society that is changing, the role of the educator also has to change. It actually has already started.

As we have discussed in each of the principles, the instructor can act as a learning facilitator when inviting individuals to pause and reflect to find their answers (the principles Reflection and of Tacit Knowledge) instead of jumping into the traditional role of sage on the stage. We can help the traditionally passive audience to become personally engaged and excited by helping them identify what they want to know. We need to establish what their questions are, and what passions or context drive them (principles of Relevance and Integration), instead of assuming we are the experts and they are a tabula rasa.

Vivien: I have become increasingly aware of how this trend is emerging from the world of corporate education, where coaches, mentors and leadership development programs seek to engage the individuals in a way that is far more participative and democratic than we traditionally see it in educational institutions.

Indeed, and this[11] is of particular value when we consider that the goal of management education[12] is to equip the leaders of tomorrow, who can address our social and environmental challenges with a different level of self-confidence, consciousness, and hopeful excitement.

Julia: Summarizing then, this is the last principle but clearly not the least, since an expert in facilitating learning has the power to make all the difference and to implement the previous nine.

Andres: The key to be an effective learning facilitator is in understanding that we are there not to teach, but to help others learn.

Nick: This shift in how we see ourselves is accompanying an evolution in society, with its trend to more democratic, participatory, and empowered attitudes. It reflects an evolution from domination to partnership models, as some scholars have noted.

Vivien: Yes, I believe this is what is needed to maximize the contribution of the instructors to the learning process. We need to unleash the potential of the younger generation; to be facilitators of their own learning and of their holistic development.

This is a good lead into the next section, where we will explore what is the impact and consequences of having such a different approach in responsible management education, and what the new roles and goals are for educators.

PART 3

So What Is the Impact?

CHAPTER 16

Different Roles for a Teacher

The last principle of the previous section referred to the Learning Facilitator, a new approach to the traditional role of the educator. While teaching has been widely centered on telling, a one-way communication through lectures and master classes, the "sage on the stage" model has been increasingly questioned as an appropriate pedagogical approach, and we are witnessing a transition toward the "guide on the side." Perhaps a better role needed from the 21st-century educator is to facilitate learning. But what does learning facilitation look like?

When we talk about "learning facilitation," the first conceptual shift is that the focus is on the *learning*, and not on the teaching.[1] It concerns what happens to the student, rather than what the instructor has to transmit. The student is not the fortuitous—and passive—recipient of the flow of information and knowledge emerging from an expert's mind. The student is in fact the client, the guest to be served, the one who has to find a benefit in the experience.

As we discussed before, the global access to instant information has also transformed the value added by the instructor. Information and materials are no longer the privilege of the expert, due to up-to-date information all students have at their fingertips.[2] Instructional videos on YouTube teach any discipline we can dream of, and we can select the preferred style of the instructor. Google Scholar will list top-ranked latest research on any topic, and free Massive Open Online Courses (MOOCs) from Ivy League schools are available to anyone.

If delivery of content is no longer the value added, what can a learning facilitator do to contribute value, relevance, and excitement to the learning experience?

There are three roles for a learning facilitator: (a) Designer, (b) Instructor, and (c) Coach or Mentor.

a. The Designer role involves identifying the learning outcomes, and selecting the pedagogical approaches and techniques to best meet those outcomes. As we have seen in the previous section, the learning principles provide a guide for designing powerful learning interventions. When designing a class, the facilitator can consider how to ensure it is relevant to the students; that their tacit knowledge is brought into the room and social learning is promoted; that activities are selected to uncover paradigms and to help shift mental models; that students are seen as holistic learners; that the classroom is a safe and appreciative environment; that reflection is promoted; that contents are linked to develop self-awareness; and, finally, that a systems perspective pervades the contents.[3]

b. The Instructor role is the most familiar one, and it refers to selecting materials, sharing information, and training students by providing exercises and techniques they will find valuable in promoting their learning. However, this role needs to be revisited too, as the perception of value added is shifting.

What is the unique expertise that we have as educators, which would be most valuable for the students? What can we share and present that could not be found as easily on the Internet, and that might be more complete or updated, better illustrated, or more practical? Late American educator Donald Finkel[4] from the progressive Evergreen State College shares in his book *Teaching with your mouth shut* that lectures don't promote learning because they are focused on sharing conclusions, and that they leave the audience in a passive mindset. If the lecturer is charismatic, the participants may give their full attention—but, ironically, may be left feeling such admiration for someone perceived as really superior, and they might be dazzled by the presentation rather than by the content. Many educators observe that contents learned via reading or lectures tend to fade rapidly. Information provided orally is hard to remember, and therefore students take notes, paying more attention to capture what is being said than to reflecting and making meaning out of it. Exams are meant to ensure that students "learned" what was told to them, but as Finkel observes, "how many could pass those same exams without any subsequent preparation, five years later?" What is the point of testing memory on something that will be forgotten soon after?

When teachers present a topic to the class, the reflection is made by the speaker, and not by the audience. According to educator John Dewey, the best learning is inquiry-based and experiential. If we would learn by simply being told, Finkel reflects, parents would have a much easier time as they tell their children all the time what they need to do or how to be. In addition, our current student population has very short attention spans. How to use the expertise and knowledge of the instructor, then? Finkel suggests that we carefully design experiences for the students, where they can discuss, examine, analyze, share, and collectively produce insights. This pedagogic technique is inquiry-based[5] and is the essence of methodologies such as Action Research or Action Learning. More recently, this approach is known as Problem-Based Learning (PBL) and Issue-Centric learning. The common characteristic is that instead of organizing a class around a content that has to be taught, it is organized around problems that have to be solved. Problems that qualify for this type of pedagogy are complex, and are not technical problems solvable with one answer. They require analysis, critical reflection, imagination, research, systems thinking, and collaboration, plus specific information or mastery of contents, which then are sought by the students in a just-in-time way—by going on Google or asking some expert. For example, one problem might be how to design our city for the future. To tackle this problem, students in a business school would have to find information about climate change in their region, urban planning, politics, governmental regulations, economics, health impacts, diversity and inclusion, among other disciplines that may be systemically relevant. Because students are engaged in solving the problem, they will naturally search for information that will help them in their journey. The learning facilitator then, much as a corporate team coach, will periodically intervene with a "just-in-time" concept or tool that can help the students to overcome obstacles hindering their progress. The goal is not to rob the learning from the learners, but to instead offer timely input when needed. This is, after all, how we have successfully learned throughout our life; trying to solve a problem we encountered, we pondered, planned, and took effective actions, which became more easily assimilated in our memory.

> ## A Story
>
> PBL was first developed at McMaster University Medical School in Canada in the 1960s, and has since been extensively used in higher education.[6] It does not require a transformation of the whole institution and its curriculum (although it could be an interesting option). Finkel used the PBL approach when he developed a course called *Political Ecology*, where students learned economics and biology as they wrestled with the problem of reconciling economic prosperity and environmental projection. In another PBL course, called *Health: Individual and Community*, students master contents of biology, psychology, anthropology, and sociology as they attempt to discover new ways to conceive health care.

The learning principles are also a useful guide when wearing the Instructor hat. As a checklist, the following questions can help ensure we are creating the best learning environment:

1. Is what I am about to tell really *relevant* to the students—from their perspective?
2. Have I checked the extent of their *tacit knowledge*—what they already may know or think about this topic?
3. Am I presenting my content in a concise way and in a form that challenges their *mental models*?
4. Have I found some moments to embed *reflection* into my lecturette?
5. Is my input providing a *systemic perspective* of the topic?
6. Is what I am about to tell them not something that would be more beneficial to their learning were they to find it out by themselves?

7. Am I helping connect with *feelings* and meaning-making?

8. Have I planned some ways to *reinforce* the learnings of today's session?

While the traditional instructor role is reduced in this new approach, another role is greatly expanded:

c. The Coaching and Mentoring role. The learning facilitator can make a valuable contribution to the students' learning by offering brief individual or collective coaching, and mentoring support. This can take the shape of asking thought-provoking questions, challenging their perspectives, having an inquiry attitude that fosters clear elaboration of their thinking; providing detailed feedback on their writing or their participation; or inviting them to identify—and then answer—their own questions.

A Story

Inspired by Finkel, I changed the way I guided reflection on readings. Instead of providing some questions the students had to answer (What did you find intriguing? What did you like? What was new for you? How did this relate to your life or experience?)—I invited the students to identify one question the reading generated for them, and to write a short essay about it. This created a situation where they didn't know the answer, and had to process and develop their own insights. I must say that the instruction was not easy for the students to understand, given that they are trained to respond to questions testing their understanding, rather than thinking of their own questions—and answering them! However, the results were far richer and more profound than when they just answered my question. This simple change helped ensure maximum relevance of their learning for each student. It also helped them to gain access to, and build on, their tacit knowledge, combining it with self-directed learning as they sought for answers.

The learning principles can also be a helpful guide to educators wearing the coaching or mentoring hat, like in the following checklist:

1. Am I planning to ask challenging questions, to take them out of their comfort zone? (This might force them to confront unfamiliar realities and unanticipated possibilities, and thereby help the students confront their assumptions and reflex thinking.)
2. When providing feedback, am I enhancing their self-awareness using an appreciative tone?
3. Am I introducing some triggers for reflection when I am mentoring students, instead of simply telling them my point of view—and, thus, in a sense, rob them of their own learning?

These are examples of questions that can prompt new insights from the students, and the selection of the most fitting approaches will be an important judgment made by the learning facilitator.

A frequently raised concern when discussing the new learning facilitation role is that students may have some knowledge, but the fact that they enroll in a program means that they have more to learn. This is not only a reality but also their expectation. How do learning facilitators "facilitate" learning when the students simply don't know what they don't know?

To address this question, we can find the following chart helpful.

Q1 "I know what I don't know": *Make space for their questions. Make it relevant.*	Q2 "I know what I know": *Have her teach, share or present. Create social learning opportunities.*
Q4 "I don't know what I don't know": *Introduce concepts, make Just-in-time interventions, help them link the new with their world. Make it relevant.*	Q3 "I don't know what I know": *Ask them, give them prompts to reflect. Help them find their tacit knowledge.*

Quadrant 1 describes participants who realize they don't know much about a topic, are curious about it, or unsure of their understanding. The learning facilitator can explore what questions the participants have about a theme, to promote ownership of the learning, and to make the experience relevant, based on the stated interests of the students in the room.

Quadrant 2 describes participants who have knowledge about a topic, and are aware of it. They know what they know, although it may not always be obvious for the instructor. After asking what questions they have about a topic, and before jumping to answer them, the learning facilitator can first seek what knowledge is in the room, and then create opportunities for students to share what they know. This can include having them teach or present it, in a dialogue, in small groups, or with Learning Partners. They become valuable moments of Social Learning in action.

Quadrant 3 describes Tacit Knowledge: when participants are not conscious of what they know. After asking what questions they have about a topic, or when introducing it, the learning facilitator can pause before sharing his expertise, and ask everyone to take a moment and write down some possible thoughts about that topic or question. The silent time will allow everyone to seek any available knowledge they may have, therefore helping the participants connect with their tacit knowledge.

Finally, **Quadrant 4** describes the most traditional situation, when the participants don't know what they don't know. This may be the most frequent assumption of instructors, and it is worthwhile to take a moment and confirm this is the case. Once it is clear that the participants do not know about a topic, the learning facilitator can wear his "instructor hat" and present the new contents. This role is most powerful when the instructor introduces contents following a clue—for example, it may be important information for a given project the participants are working on, or for a discussion that is underway. In other words, when it is "just-in-time" information that illuminates a possible way to go, as opposed to "just-in-case" information that the student might have a need for at an unspecified time in the future.

For many instructors, it may sound strange to think of reserving the "teaching" to the occurrence of a "just-in-time" opportunity, as opposed to a well-planned session. But it may become more understandable if we consider a new way of designing the whole learning experience. Experienced facilitators of learning are able to anticipate "just-in-time" opportunities and be prepared. And if that opportunity doesn't occur, they can let their preparation go and go with the flow.

CHAPTER 17

The Flipped Classroom and What It Takes

Part of the new approach to learning is to lessen the one-way flow of information from expert to student, and for the expert to center on the learner. When the educator, as part of the designed lesson plan, deliberately chooses to refrain from using lecturing as the sole means of teaching, she can replace it with another powerful action: to hold the space of listening.[1] This action inverts the traditional approach to education, creating what is called the "flipped classroom," a term coined in 2012 by American chemistry teachers Jonathan Bergmann and Aaron Sams.[2] They converted a lecture-based class into a participatory setting with a simple inversion. Instead of asking students to listen to lectures and do homework to apply what was taught, they provided students with materials and videos to watch in between classes, and used the classroom time to dialogue and work collaboratively on problems. They found a deeper learning and improved grades as a result, and the concept has since spread outside the United States.

Finkel notes that the conceptual shift from teaching to facilitating learning may pose a challenge both to the instructor and to the students. The tendency to rely on opinions of powerful others is something that originates in our first years of life, when we depend for survival on some almighty adults who know how to take care of all our needs. That expectation lingers under the surface throughout our life, repeated in expectations toward our bosses, politicians, spouses, doctors, or—teachers!

This means that students may have to learn a new way of participating, of taking full ownership of their learning. It also means that educators have to review their own habits, teaching methodologies, and instincts. It will not be easy going against the grain at first, but the benefits do not take long to manifest themselves. Professor Anthony Buono, at Bentley

University, describes his initial struggle as he explored the role of learning facilitator in an undergraduate course. He found that, as he intentionally set aside his customary role of expert, the result was an unnerving silence from the class. He writes of wrestling to address this with his tendency to "fill in the blanks" when confronted by a lack of responsiveness from the class. He persevered, and was happy to find that the less he talked, the more the students did.

To design and facilitate learning in this way, educators may have to reflect on the meaning of power and authority in the classroom. As noted in Chapter 1, when professors in higher education are not given proper pedagogical training, many rely on teaching just as they have been taught. This means that the traditional power relationship is replicated: the expert-professor holds the power to state outcomes, to set the norms for interaction, to give assignments and grades, and to decide on the pass or fail. This gives rise to an interesting question. Is it possible that some educators, who had not had good personal experiences as students, may, on becoming the teacher in power, find a way to compensate for the frustrations of the past?

But as we have seen, the circumstances are changing. In the past the students accepted the rules of the game because they were receiving content and experience from the instructors, which they could not get in other ways. This seems to be different at the current time, since no expert can always compete with updated contents available online! The interesting cultural shift is from power to authority, where, for educators, respect is gained when we are able to create the best learning environment, one that is empowering, exciting, motivating, engaging, relevant, and meaningful.

The learning facilitator therefore will be called to demonstrate innovative skills in class design, as well as careful and rigorous preparation. At the same time, versatility and flexibility become essential to the educators in adapting to what happens in the classroom and to consider the questions and interests of the class. If we truly believe that our focus should be on the students' learning and not, as traditionally, on the teaching of subjects, we need to pay attention to the questions in the classroom, and listen to what they are telling us. What issues are the questions raising, what is unclear, confusing, difficult to relate to, disconnected from the students' experience or reality, and challenging to their beliefs or under-standing? This may be what requires our attention, and we need to let go of our plan in order to follow where that reality is taking us. This is assuming that the questions are related to the theme, at least in the mind of the students. It may not seem obvious or important for the educator, but they need to be listened to carefully. And if we cannot alter our plan, we need to find a way to attend to those questions, because ignoring them will not make them disappear.

Other competencies important for effective learning facilitation are those related with creating democratic and participatory environments, an appreciative atmosphere in the classroom and empowering interactions, which will be the new added value of educators. While it may seem that relinquishing power would undermine the importance of the learning facilitator's presence in the flipped classroom, ironically, just the opposite occurs. By role-modeling a "white-belt" attitude, the educator opens a different environment for learning, one where students are empowered, coached, mentored, and the learning happens for everyone—educator included. The educator who talks less, is more listened to, and is granted the respect of her authority, as she adds wisdom to knowledge.

Finkel, addressing an understandable concern of some educators, observes that as the educator tries to create a democratic setting in the classroom, she will not lose authority, and will never be seen as the stu-dents' equal. The difference is that she can make the students aware of their recurrent, spontaneous tendency to seek an all-knowing authority, which is equal to granting power to the expert while abdicating the own power. Becoming aware of that unconscious pattern we all carry from our childhood is already a great learning gift. The intentional abdication of "expert" power in no way equates to loss of authority. Indeed, discover-ing that we as educators can earn even greater authority by intentionally "letting go" of the familiar trappings of our power can be a step in our personal development.

It is interesting how little research is focused on this power shift in the classroom that the new generation is calling for.[3] While there are plenty of resources available addressing how to innovate in business school or higher education teaching; incorporate technology, creativity, prag-matism; use ethical or sustainability lenses into all we teach; and make e-learning and virtual classrooms good learning experiences, there is very little exploration of the challenges in the power relationship in the classroom. A literature review on power and authority in the classroom brings up mostly governance issues, discrimination and egalitarian education, tensions between authorities and educators, affirmative action and power understood differently by men and by women, but leaves unexplored the changing power dynamics in the teacher–student relationship for the new generation. Most importantly, in a context that might be seen as restricting and questioning teachers' traditional power, we are failing to notice the new developmental opportunities opening up for teachers. Significantly, we ignore the benefits of experimenting how to approach power—such as converting "power over" into "empowering other," thus increasing respect and developing professional and moral authority vis-à-vis the students.

This said, it is clear that both teachers and students need to make the shift. There are few chances that this will happen spontaneously, and it is unlikely that students will overwhelmingly demand it from their teachers. Too many years of behavioral conditioning have shaped our young into individuals with unquestioned acceptance of the status quo. To navigate through formal education, they have learned what gets rewarded, and what to avoid. But, is this the attitude we want to foster in the generation that will have to start solving the problems we have created? How is our pedagogical approach developing empowered men and women, who can become self-aware and confident, engaged and proactive? Given that the future is shaped by the new trends and not by old habits, we, the educators, should consider that we need to adapt to our students' world, rather than the other way around. For the greater benefit of both.

CHAPTER 18

Evaluating Results

A Story

When I took on my first teaching job, at the undergraduate level of a School of Tourism in the Universidad del Salvador, in Buenos Aires, Argentina, I faced a dilemma. How could I honor the principle that individuals learn more when they take full ownership of their learning, and at the same time fulfill the task of grading their performance, which from the perspective of intrinsic motivation and accountability was a contradiction? I decided to try out self-grading, and shared with the students from the start what the criteria would be. I was not able to compare the results with any other benchmark, but the engagement during the course was high. The group of over 40 students participated actively and worked enthusiastically on their projects, and at the final session I had an unexpected surprise: One student failed himself, something I would not have done considering his performance. I asked him for the reason, and he said that he realized he had not taken advantage of the materials, he had not allocated sufficient time to this subject. He had realized the content of the course (Marketing for Tourism) was very important for his future, so he decided to do the whole course again.

How we go about evaluating the learning is indeed a dilemma for instructors, particularly for those who feel comfortable with more participative learning settings, those who seek to fully empower the students, and definitely when we consider the Learning Principles suggested in Part Two, all based on well-researched disciplines. It becomes a contradiction to promote self-directed learning, foster students setting their personal learning goals to develop ownership of the learning process, focus on facilitating learning, and then step into a more traditional "power-over" method of deciding who receives what grade.

Certainly students will not question why we switch into a different position, because they are used to it, but the act of grading is not an isolated event at the end of a term: it is a process that influences and conditions the whole student–teacher relationship.

When we start a course inviting students to identify their personal learning goals within the boundaries of the subject, we are setting the stage for a different learning experience. We are giving the message that they are the center of the attention, not us, and we are there to help them in their learning journey. This message may sound trivial, or even known as listed in the school's philosophy and values, but it becomes real when behaviors that are new and unusual take place in the classroom.

The Personal Learning Goals are an example of such new behaviors. Students are pushed to pause and reflect what they want to get out of the course, and we can invite them to state the goals at the level of knowing, doing and being. They may not know what they don't know, but this is not an obstacle, since the fact of being invited to reflect is already an important shift in the power relationship. The goals should furthermore be specific, measurable, aligned with the scope of the program, realistic, and time based.[1]

Another unusual teacher initiative that shapes a different learning environment is to introduce how progress and results will be assessed. We then invite students to list the criteria that should be used to measure progress and learning. It is important to explain why we decided to do it this way: because we believe that students can have a valid perspective to set the criteria, and when collectively agreed, it becomes a more powerful foundation for learning. It reinforces the role of the teacher as a learning facilitator, and the importance we see in students owning their learning. I certainly have my own list of criteria in mind, and if one criterion I consider essential is not listed by the students, I can suggest adding it.

In addition to agreeing on the criteria, students define the grading scale: What do we need to do to get an F, D, C, B, or A? This exercise is experienced as a fun moment, at the same time it establishes how they are going to assess their progress and achievements. In order for this to be a developmental scorecard and not a onetime exercise, the learning facilitator will need to periodically bring up the scorecard, ask the students to check for themselves how they are doing, and to think what they need to do more or differently in order to achieve their goals (and the desired grades). This is a different position than telling them that if they don't submit the next assignment they will get an F.

Participating actively in identifying the criteria has been seen as an effective way to avoid grade inflation, since students are not left to their subjective perception but are basing their grading on agreed upon factors.

Acting as a learning facilitator has many characteristics of a coaching or mentoring role, and it may require paying attention to the individual performance of the students along the course, reaching out individually to help them remember their scorecard and decide what to do about it. I do not visibly "police" them, but I set up a tracking table to have an updated picture of what each one is doing in terms of the criteria, and periodically reach out. Frequently the reactions of students are to apologize, and promise "I will post it tomorrow." This is a teaching moment— when the learning facilitator needs to remind the student that she doesn't have to promise anything, because it is not "for the teacher" that she will do it, but for herself. Telling students that they learn for their own good is something common, but acting according to it is what makes it real. Educator Peter Finkel observes that a closed door is a better message than a "do not enter" sign.

The difficulty around changing the traditional way of evaluating is possibly related to the understanding that assessing learning and grading are essential components of the teacher's role and responsibility.[2] This seems to be an assumption not shared by students, as a 2004 case study of 480 students reveals. When asked if "Because of self-grading (they) felt the instructor was not fulfilling his duty as a teacher," 92.2 percent disagreed or strongly disagreed, 5.8 percent felt that self-grading made no difference, and only 1.9 percent agreed or strongly agreed with the statement.[3]

The same study found that self-grading improved the students' motivation, and they indicated feeling a greater responsibility for their own learning, something that was corroborated in other studies.[4] Even students who participated in the weighing of their assessment factors showed a higher sense of control and performance.

Self-assessment has extensively been indicated as a valuable process in higher education, for students to identify the gap between their current knowledge and skills and their goal. This is not only a cognitive skill but also requires reflexivity and commitment, as noted by several scholars.[5] It has been noted by several scholars that when given the option, some students choose not to self-assess, or are reluctant to do so. The reasons found are lack of skills or confidence,[6] preferring to be assessed by experts,[7] cultural issues or fear of being too harsh on themselves,[8] and fear of being wrong.[9]

An alternative to self-grading has also been used,[10] in view of the fact that students rarely use their graded exams to learn from them. Replacing traditional grading, the tests are returned to students with marks of "right" or "wrong," and the students have to learn from their mistakes, figuring out what was wrong and how to correct it. They can then resubmit their tests, and earn half of their points back.

Other alternatives to instructor grading are group, or peer grading, where classmates provide feedback and help each other improve. This approach can benefit from a good role modeling by the instructor on providing behavior-based feedback, where the strengths and the opportunities are both indicated, without making judgments about the author.

This points back to a previously considered question: What are the results we are seeking in the teaching process? That students learn, develop, or that they earn certain grades? Professional educators and educational psychologists have repeatedly asserted that too much emphasis is placed on extrinsic motivators, such as grades. What is being rewarded in those cases is performance on a test or during a course, which does not necessarily imply the students learned.[11] When students grade themselves they learn to play a different role, becoming actors of their own development. This requires that faculty step back from a traditional grading task and open up new possibilities of interaction. In fact, grading tends to drop in importance as part of the instructor's role, and helping learn becomes the focus. But this leads us to ponder the question once again: What is the ultimate purpose of instructors? What is their *raison d'être*?

CHAPTER 19

Going Back to the Purpose

Critical Reflection Theory invites us to develop critical thinking in our students, and that should also apply to ourselves as educators. Why are we doing what we are doing, anyway? Frequently we see the answer to this question in the learning outcomes defined for each subject: The purpose is that students learn how to develop a business strategy; how to analyze market trends; how to read a balance sheet; how to motivate employees; how to set up a new process; learn the economic theories that shape our transactions or the regulatory frameworks that organize them.

But if we ask the question again, we get to a deeper level of meaning. What is the purpose of knowing all that? What are the ultimate aims in the level of being and doing? What are we preparing our students for, in a larger picture, one that addresses the use of their unique skills as actors and shapers of a world in flux?

We may have come this far to realize that in our practice as educators these questions need to be answered first, because they impact the concrete learning outcomes we choose for our classes, and therefore the contents and the pedagogical approaches that best fit. Posing these questions to ourselves as educators also automatically lifts us into a higher dimension of contribution and purpose.

It is common to hear that faculty have to give information to undergraduates, and enable graduates to analyze information. In the protected environment of the educational institution, the world from outside is brought in the shape of subjects and domains of knowledge for in-depth scrutiny. But, as a student observed once in response to a case study he had not prepared for, how would reading a case help him get ready for addressing real-life challenges? In the problems he had to face daily, the information is not lined up in 10 pages, but scattered; what stakeholders think comes with body language and tones that convey a unique meaning to the words. There is no linear story to analyze, but fragments of information that need to be connected, sorted through, and made sense of. There is a multidimensional context (social, financial, political, legal, historical, cultural, religious, humanistic, etc.) coloring the scenes, and on top everything may even be impacted by the events of the day, or the mood and the health of the person. Indeed, real-life problems are never a rational challenge to be solved like a puzzle, with logic, devoid of emotions and empathy. As a matter of fact, we would question the leadership competencies of anyone who would propose a solution based on such a robot-like thinking.

While we carefully design a lesson-plan, something different happens outside the classroom. Young people are digital natives who absorb and use information at a speed we can hardly follow. They are immersed in a world that offers them 24/7 connection to anyone—anywhere. They may accept the "chalk and talk," but they really do not need teachers as providers of information. Memorizing facts, theories, and formulas has a different value when information is available anytime on a portable device, and more up to date. "I am surprised," a colleague recently commented, "students are bringing information into the class that I had no idea about!" Should we be surprised that they are not more engaged when real life has such a different pace and content outside of the school's walls?

We are living in what is called the VUCA world: volatile, uncertain, complex, and ambiguous. A few decades ago, the uncertainty of a young person trying to understand a situation was calmed by some older or more experienced mentor, one who knew the "ropes" and could provide adequate guidance. But the "this-is-how-things-are-done-here" is a formula that expired and has lost its comforting value—other than to learn from the consequences. What worked before is no longer a recipe for what can work now, and in many cases may even be at the root of the problems we have to solve today. The increasing information available on the environmental and social impacts of our way of life is indicating that the products we manufacture, consume, and dispose of have to radically change, be reinvented and redesigned to make our life sustainable on the planet—not to mention if we want a flourishing earth. And it is not only about products and services: The challenges span over where we live, how we travel, communicate, eat, work out, take care of our health, entertain ourselves, connect to each other, and find fulfillment.

The situations our students will have to address are what are known as "wicked problems," with no right or wrong answers. They involve stakeholders we never thought of, like Nature or the next generations. In addition, the landscape is changing at such a pace that we can no longer aim at preparing students for a job that probably will be very different in one decade, or even not exist anymore. What then are we preparing our students for?

Research and management education scholars have been giving extended attention to this question, seeking to identify what skills, knowledge, and competencies are needed today and in times to come. With some variances, scholars agree that the skills for the 21st century are not centered on specific knowledge, but on critical thinking about information. To know data is of little value if students cannot extract meaning out of them, nor make connections with the context in which they are living.[1] Events need to be debriefed to learn from them, to capitalize on what went well or badly if we want to avoid a thoughtless repetition of wrongdoings. The ability to inquire and challenge in a way that creates bridges of understanding, rather than rifts of disconnection and polarization among individuals, is a skill that can be of the greatest value in negotiations or decision making.

We need a society of individuals able to understand themselves and uncover their own assumptions and habits of mind; who are aware of their cognitive and emotional bias and interpretations. We need young people who can develop their own perspectives listening and integrating the points of views of others; and who can communicate their thoughts in a clear way. Although many have grown up in a predominantly individualistic society, the uncharted territory facing us requires team players, individuals able to and interested in collaborating with others to find unseen solutions. The problems are too big and complex to be solved single-handedly. Creativity, the ability to integrate right- and left-brain capacities and to think diagonally* will be key competencies to bring forth all the innovation we will need.

---

* Thanks to Pablo Altieri for the concept of Diagonal Thinking. www.diagonal-minds.com

Transferable skills are a good option—but developing lifelong learners is even better. The responsible management of any profession will require to look beyond "what is good for me," and to transcend even the next stage—"what is good for us?" starting to ask "What is good for them?" For others, for all? *Because ignoring stakeholders will become a liability, a costly mistake, a serious strategic error.*

Some years ago I was facing the challenge of how to develop the students' systems thinking. Then a volcano by the name of Eyjafjallajökull erupted in Iceland, creating a cloud of ash that disrupted the flights within, from, and to Europe for five days, launching the highest travel disruption since the Second World War. Passengers in cities around the world had their plans altered, meetings cancelled, and were facing unexpected costs and a variety of personal life impacts—all because of the plume of a volcano in a country many were not able to pinpoint on the map. I needed no textbook to teach systemic interconnections, and the students learned how we are all part of a web of life.

In a similar way, teaching the importance of considering all stakeholders when designing products or services, when developing a strategic plan and even when consuming is no longer a teachers' challenge. We just have to look at any newspaper, and start identifying how the problems of today can be traced back to some myopic decisions of yesterday, that missed including some stakeholders' perspectives, interests, or needs. Then do a numeric estimation of the costs incurred by that oversight.

The world has changed, and the pyramid of power (a few on the top holding the power) that has been the organizing model for 5,000 years of civilization is collapsing. Scholar and author Raimundo Panikkar indicates that the future will not be a new, big tower of power, but a networked society, with "well trodden paths from house to house." This is happening already with the help of universally available information—thanks to technology and social media. What some were able to do in the past, and go unnoticed because the impact or consequences of their decisions would not be easily seen, or would not become public or obvious, is becoming more and more a rare exception. To begin with, we are able to witness—and suffer from—many consequences of the behaviors of the past, be it in the quality of the air we breathe, in climate-related events, or in social unrest. The connection between cause and effect has been shortened. Secondly, everyone has become a potential journalist behind a phone, getting the news out in 140 characters and with a click. We have more opportunities to learn from others, to get inspired, and encouraged, just as the first wave of the Arab Spring initially demonstrated, because we are more exposed to what others are doing on a planet with fewer disconnected parts.

As the web linking us gets tighter, we all become more visible members of society. What we individually do, even in the privacy of our kitchen, matters, and that awareness is expanding. What in the past was an unquestioned behavior, like eating meat or using plastic bags to carry our groceries, has become a questioned habit, or even a small personal feeling of "wrong." This means that when we stand in a class thinking of how to develop responsible leaders, we need to address values, habits, patterns of decision and consumption, economic paradigms, and their impacts on us. We need to create a space to dialogue about us as emotional beings, as humans with a desire of purpose and meaning. We need to have conversations about how we are caught up in and are personally fostering a culture of "doing" to "have more" so we can "be" happy, with the characteristic that once we have one desired object, the craving for the next object begins. That is called addiction.

So what is the role educators want to play to create a generation of global responsible leaders? What is the ultimate purpose of educators in our current time? Every educator has to reflect and find his or her own answer to this question. But we may have a unique opportunity to help shape the new accelerators of change. It may require some changes in ourselves, but they may be easier than they seem. And, as a matter of fact, many people are already acting in very new ways.

CHAPTER 20

Developing Change Accelerators

In different parts of the world, pioneering adult educators have listened to the murmurs of change and are experimenting with very different ways of organizing higher education.[1] In the city of Nancy,[2] France, an alliance was formed in 1999 between a business school, an engineering university, and a college of arts, with the visionary purpose of developing individuals with a multidisciplinary perspective, one that includes art, science, technology, and management, because, the educators reasoned, the complex challenges require an interdisciplinary preparation. The collaboration is implemented through shared courses and projects, and also through issuing joint degrees.

In a similar way, the Worcester Polytechnic Institute in Massachusetts, United States, experimented with a course for undergraduates, titled Leadership, Creativity, Innovation, and Entrepreneurship, which has been created and is taught by the deans from Humanities, Engineering, and Business. The course helps students understand the complexity and multidisciplinary approach necessary for finding solutions to the big problems we face, such as food and energy supply, healthcare quality and delivery, and global sustainability. Beyond this, the school has a long tradition of using problem-based learning, and students select among many national and international locations to work on a project for several weeks.

An example of problem-based learning but centered in a local community is Leuphana University in Lüneburg, Germany, where students enrolled in the Masters in Sustainability Science are invited to undertake a transdisciplinary project looking at ways in which their city administration can contribute to creating a sustainable community and city. Students learn to work with individuals outside the world of academia, and faculty ensures that they take time to reflect on the learning process itself.

Concerned with the urgent needs of solutions in so many areas of our planet, the University of Vermont, United States, created the Sustainable Entrepreneurship MBA, and, influenced by Stuart Hart, avoided creating the "saddle effect" (where sustainability courses are simply added to a traditional program). Instead, the curriculum of the MBA is focused on developing entrepreneurs prepared to create business solutions at the base of the income pyramid (BoP), addressing the world's 4 billion poorest. The accelerated one-year program includes a practicum where the partic000ipants work in one of the 18 international hubs of the Base of the Pyramid network on real projects. The aim of this program is to develop an "ecosystem approach" to innovation in business, where every stakeholder (including nature and the next generations) is served. An example of such an ecosystem approach is CleanStar Mozambique, a BoP venture that provides clean cooking solutions that eliminate indoor air pollution in urban households. The biofuel is produced in a local refinery using crops supplied by subsistence farmers who learned to set up a multicrop sus000tainable agriculture. The practice allowed them to raise both their income and food security while producing excess cassava that serves as feedstock. And the circular solution reduced the charcoal used for cook stoves, which accounts for a significant part of the deforestation and greenhouse gas emissions in the region. The MBA program develops skills to conceive this kind of ecosystem innovative solutions.

Another innovation in pedagogical methods, connecting learning with addressing real needs in the developing world, is found under the pio000neering leadership of Professor Henrietta Onwuegbuzie at Lagos Business School in Nigeria. In her school, community challenges are assigned to first-year students, and the courses they attend focus on them learning how to develop their project and provide solutions to the challenge with an ongoing reporting process to a mentor. At the graduate level, students create a profitable social enterprise during the semester with a starting loan of $40 which she gives to them. The students have to find a way to create value for the community through a service or a product, return the loan with interest, and earn a profit. The young participants initially see this as an impossible task, but are able to find creative ways to set up their initiatives, which in many cases continue after the course. What is being taught is that with creativity and listening to the local needs, very little capital can be enough to start a profitable enterprise. As an example, one student who had web design skills saw carpenters selling their furniture pieces on the roadside. He created a website to sell their products, and ship it nationwide. The carpenters were able to get more orders, build their own workshops, and raise their income—in some cases, employing more workers. The initiative was copied by Professor Amelia Naim in Jakarta, Indonesia, although she gave only $15 as initial capital. Interestingly, some students actually returned the money because they didn't even need it to create a business.

We can see how several people have realized the importance of bringing the reality of the most serious needs of our planet into the classroom. To develop globally responsible leaders at the Center for the Advancement of Sustainable Enterprise, Colorado State University, United States, students work during the 18 months of the program building businesses at the Bottom of the Pyramid. They develop solutions to meet their "clients'" needs and spend 8 to 10 weeks abroad during the summer semester.

What this shows is that issue-centered learning, problem-based learning, action learning, and experiential learning are different names for an approach that seeks to convert the siloed, fragmented list of subjects into a flow of accessible knowledge that is as multidisciplinary as the problems of life themselves are.

Some initiatives pay particular attention to the mindset that needs to be developed for responsible leadership, a mindset[3] that is different from past stances. The Lancaster University Management School, at McGill University in Canada, for example, focuses on developing five mindsets: a "worldly" perspective; analytical and reflective skills; collaboration, and proactivity. Directed toward managers with work experience, the International Masters in Practicing Management is held in partnership with colleges in five locations: England, Canada, India, China, and Brazil. Each school hosts a module of 10 days that is based on a different mindset and the participants set the learning goals and context based on their own organizational or business challenges. This aspect speaks to the principle of Relevance, as the contents are tailored to address the participants' concrete needs. Social Learning is also present in this program, since the participants share and transfer knowledge to their colleagues, learning from each other's experience and insights, thus changing the traditional power structure of expert over student. In a program designed as a sequenced learning experience (principle of Repetition and Reward), between modules the managers seek to apply the newly gained concepts and perspectives, and as they reunite for the next module, they share how they tried to put new ideas into practice. The program also includes journaling, and the managers reflect on what they are learning about themselves and about the experience, which is a way to enact the principles of Tacit Knowledge and Self-Awareness. The innovative design of the program reflects the imprint of management guru Henry Mintzberg and his experiences with Action Reflection Learning (ARL) at the MiL Institute in Sweden, where they have been using a similar design for in-company leadership development programs.

The Vicens Vives Program at ESADE, in Catalonia, Spain, also targets young professionals with management experience, with the goal of developing similar characteristics: reflective, creative and critical thinking, and self-awareness. Using current sociopolitical, technical, economic, and cultural challenges as the arena for learning, students engage in personal reflection and debates on questions such as "What world and what country do we live in?" and "How can we improve it?" The overarching purpose is to develop leaders committed to addressing the big world problems.

These are exactly the questions Professor Ross McDonald from the University of Auckland Business School, New Zealand, present to his students. McDonald was concerned with identifying what would be the best method to engage young people in changing the world for the better. His goal is to educate "for" responsibility, and to this end he finds it helpful to integrate emotions, personal reflection, observation, and collaborative action, plus continuing exchange among peers. He indicates that responsibility is "the ability to skillfully respond to the demands of the world in ways that facilitate a maximally harmonious thriving." This requires that we expand the scope of care; if we only care about ourselves, it creates problems in the community, friends, and family. If we think only about our own class, tribe, or gender, we create conflict with those outside that boundary. If we only think of our generation's needs, we will be worsening the problems that some decades of self-indulgence have created. Thus, his perspective is that development should expand the boundaries of care. He includes emotions and values in his classes, because climate science data are no longer impersonal facts: climate has become personal and needs to be addressed as such. Students start developing their own vision of what a better world would look like. After agreeing on one vision, they identify the values needed to build that world, and finally reflect and work toward translating this into their personal responsibility, into their decisions and choices.

One pioneer in the educational philosophy of "Change starts within" is Maharishi University of Management (MUM), founded in 1971 by Maharishi Mahesh Yogi, a leading scientist of consciousness and scholar of the Vedic tradition of enlightenment, the most ancient tradition of knowledge. The University, based in Iowa, is known for its commitment to Consciousness-Based[SM] Education (CBE), a pedagogical approach centered on whole student learning (Principle Integration). Knowledge is seen as vital to the educational process, but not useful until the students are able to connect the information with how it relates to them as a person (Principle Self-Awareness), and why it is useful for the world (which reflects the principle of Relevance). One of the key methodologies used in CBE is Transcendental Meditation (TM) that research has shown to improve the cognitive functioning of the brain and is the foundation for creativity and intelligent action.[4] At Maharishi University, TM is a regular practice of students and faculty. The result of this approach is that students are able to learn at high speed and assimilate greater quantities of information compared to traditional educational systems. MUM unfolds in students the vast creative potentials that frequently go unused in life, and is committed to sustainability for life in harmony with the natural laws, which, combined with innovative thinking, results in what our planet desperately needs. The University has been expanding and evolving, yet still maintains the original seven goals that Maharishi expressed at its inception:

1. To develop the full potential of the individual
2. To realize the highest ideal of education
3. To improve governmental achievements

4. To solve the age-old problem of crime and all behavior that brings unhappiness to our world family

5. To bring fulfillment to the economic aspirations of individuals and society

6. To maximize the intelligent use of the environment

7. To achieve the spiritual goals of humanity in this generation

Along similar lines, Schumacher College was founded in 1990 in Dartington, Totnes, UK, the city where the Transition Towns Movement originated. Inspired by economist and educator E.F. Schumacher, author of *Small Is Beautiful*, and founded by Indian peace activist Satish Kumar, the college is recognized as a cutting-edge learning center. It offers postgraduate masters in Holistic Science, Ecological Design Thinking and Economics along with short courses. The unique characteristic is their pedagogical method, which is holistic (Principle Integration), transformative (Principle Self-awareness), and anchored in sustainable living (Relevance). Learning takes place in the classroom, around a campfire, sitting in a circle (Social Learning), through individual reflection or meditation (Reflection, Tacit Knowledge), walking in Nature, or working in the gardens or the kitchen. The College has been offering inspiration through the input of intellectual leaders of our time, such as Fritjof Capra, James Lovelock, Humberto Maturana, Rupert Sheldrake, Vandana Shiva, and many others.

The personal dimension is a core component of a course to develop the Sustainability Mindset, which stands on three pillars: the being, the thinking or knowing, and the doing. Designed in 2010 for the Masters program of Hospitality and Tourism at Fairleigh Dickinson University, in New Jersey, United States, it was later tailored for the MBA at Fordham and for undergraduates across campus at Nova Southeastern University, Florida. The pillars are addressed through content areas covering Eco-literacy, Spiritual and Emotional Intelligence, and System Intelligence, anchored in collaborative innovative action projects designed to make a difference in the community. The design is fully guided by the ARL principles, and students select their topics of study, use self-directed learning to explore the themes, set their personal learning goals, and self-assess their progress, with the ongoing support and coaching of the instructor as a learning facilitator, who also acts providing input and provocative questions. Pedagogical methods include meditation, journaling, dialogues, walks in nature, exercises to engage the right brain hemisphere, learning partners, individual reflection, videos, just-in-time Internet exploration of topics, writing, interviews, passion-project work, and ongoing conversations to make meaning, extract lessons, and to debrief. Some examples of passion projects that the students engage in are the creation of a professional oath for the graduates of the Masters in Hospitality and Tourism; a Net-Impact campaign on campus to develop awareness of our ecological footprint; creating a blog to educate young mothers on sustainability resources and tips for raising their babies; and the first inventory of sustainability initiatives on campus. The slow-paced course contrasts with the students' general experience, and, in the design, resembles more closely an intense executive leadership development program. Due to its transformational impact, and in response to the interest that many instructors in business schools showed in a holistic development of students, a network of academics was formed with over 40 members in 29 universities and 22 countries. They are adapting or adopting elements of the course, exchanging best practices, and generating collaborative research. The network is called LEAP! (Leverage, Educate, Accelerate, Partner) and is the United Nations Principles for Responsible Management Education (UN PRME) Working Group on the Sustainability Mindset.

Outside of the traditional structure of management education institutions, the Barefoot College in Rajasthan, India, has to be mentioned as an inspiring and exemplary innovation to develop innovative, entrepreneurial, and empowered individuals who can immediately get into action. Founded in 1972 in rural India, the college is rooted in Gandhi's values of service and community empowerment, honoring the knowledge that villages have (Tacit Knowledge, Social Learning). Here the purpose of education is seen as helping communities support themselves (Relevance), something essential in a region where most are illiterate or semi-illiterate and live on less than $1 a day, and where the circle of poverty cannot be broken without access to education.

The College accepts individuals of all ages, gender, caste, or health conditions. It gives priority to the education of the physically impaired and lower-caste groups, to single mothers, middle-aged, and divorced women, because they need the employment opportunity and income the most.

Since 1972, more than 450 physically challenged men and women and 6,525 housewives, mothers and grandmothers, midwives, farmers, daily wage workers, and small shop keepers have been trained as Barefoot midwives, hand pump mechanics, rural entrepreneurs, Barefoot day and night school teachers, solar engineers, artisans, weavers, dentists, masons, parabolic solar cooker engineers, FM radio operators and fabricators, computer instructors, accountants, toy makers, or recycling professionals, and most of them have received training in more than one activity. By giving the underprivileged and vulnerable access to education and encouraging them to take a productive role in the community, the College develops self-confident individuals who change their own and their community's life. Some examples are applying rural traditional knowledge and skills to build homes for the homeless, collect rain water in rural schools and community where potable water sources are scarce, and to spread socioeconomic messages at the grassroots level through puppetry. Furthermore, 70 trained rural semi-illiterate women are working as Barefoot Solar Engineers in Sierra Leone and Liberia.

The unusual concept of education is summarized in the following characteristics:

- Learning and unlearning: Students and teachers learn from and with each other.
- Innovation: Everyone is expected to keep an open mind, try new and "crazy" ideas, make mistakes and try again;
- Open to all: Everyone is welcome to come, share, work, and learn;
- Learning in and for action: Valuing the dignity of labor, working with their hands and head to solve real challenges of the community;
- No certificates, degrees, or diplomas are given. Graduates become the teachers.

The college has set up eight field centers in Rajasthan and its philosophy has been copied in 14 states across India. It is a thought-provoking example of leadership education at the service of real needs.

This is just a list of examples of innovative pedagogical approaches and methods, with no intention of making it an exhaustive inventory. While innovation is not yet mainstream, there are also institutions that are influencing and shaping the direction of management education. One of them is AACSB, the Association to Advance Collegiate Schools of Business. They embedded sustainability into the eligibility criteria to be met for accreditation. To explore the dimensions of change, the AACSB invited member schools to share how they were innovating. In less than five weeks they received details of nearly 300 innovations from more than 200 institutions across 35 countries, proving the power of a commitment to make a more positive impact.*

Another example is 50+20,[5] a collaborative initiative of the *World Business School Council of Sustainable Business (WBSCSB)*, the *Globally Responsible Leadership Initiative (GRLI)*, and the *UN PRME*, focused on transforming education to make it a Management Education *for* the world. Scholars and practitioners from around the globe collaborate in creating research, models, and materials that can make management education relevant and applied, holistic and integrative, responsible and sustainable, and interdisciplinary. They state the goals of management education as three: (1) developing globally responsible leaders, (2) enabling business organizations to serve the common good, and (3) engaging in the transformation of business and the economy. Through their research and thinking, they are working with international accreditation institutions like EQUIS and AACSB, who then incorporate new criteria to prepare responsible leaders for the planet. The 50+20 initiative plays an important role as they act as a lever of change—by informing those who raise the bar and set new standards for business schools around the world to shape up. The international accreditation institution AACSB has recently considered reviewing their vision toward transforming business education for global prosperity, a statement that signifies a major leap in the historic understanding of business. They increasingly see their role as promoting innovation and amplifying impact, by connecting educational institutions—students, faculty, and administration—with business and the needs of our world.

---

* AACSB International, www.aacsb.edu/innovations-that-inspire#.Vq8k28ep-UAk.twitter

The three 50+20 stated goals—developing globally responsible leaders, enabling business organizations to serve the common good, and transforming business and the economic models are at the core of Aim2Flourish, a student-led, UN Global Compact-supported global learning initiative to discover and nominate innovative businesses that serve real needs and are profitable by doing so. The initiative was inspired by Professors David Cooperrider's and Ron Fry's investigation into Business as an Agent of World Benefit that started at Case Western Reserve University in Cleveland, Ohio, in 2002 and continues today as AIM2Flourish. Professors from around the world mentor students to identify innovative entrepreneurs in their region, who are meeting one or several of the UN Sustainable Development Goals (SDGs) through the products or services they sell in a profitable way. Aim2Flourish stories about business innovations for good are then posted in a portal and the nominated entrepreneurs are celebrated. The initiative helps develop globally responsible leaders as students discover what is possible—in terms of being a profitable business and solving some of the big problems of our time. Some students in Indonesia were so inspired by the process of interviewing business leaders that they asked their professor if they could also start a social enterprise themselves. Faculty and community members also learn about a different way of conceiving business, and investors screen the posted stories for opportunities to support and scale. The global business community witnessing this movement learns about new benchmarks, in what is termed the "virtuous circle," a social process by which no one wants to be seen as "bad" by missing the chance to "do good." This social process accelerates change, and this may be Aim2Flourish's most important consequence: transforming business and the economic model we have bought into for the past 200 years, and that is still being exported without hesitation to the developing world.

But trends are made up from behaviors, and as we have seen through the stories of these pages, something is rapidly shifting.

CHAPTER 21

Closing Remarks

We started this book promising to explore how including purpose in our actions connects with planet and with theories of learning, asking "Why do we need a change in how we are preparing the next generation of leaders?," and "How can we develop them in the most effective way so they are able to shape a world flourishing for all?" The question also was "How does learning happen best?," and *best* with this particular landscape in mind: the eco-socio-enviro-techno-spiritual turbulence.

As we became aware that a painting—from the 1800s!—could well depict many higher education classrooms of today, we knew something was amiss. Reviewing the 10 Action Reflection Learning (ARL) Principles we discovered how wisdom and knowledge, collected across centuries from a variety of disciplines and sources, can serve as a guide to educators in addressing new learning imperatives. The questions of Julia, Nick, Andres, and Vivien helped us understand how those eclectic theories, when applied in the classroom, can inform and inspire to powerful activities to develop individuals holistically. This can prepare the students for an array of unanticipated but critical tasks that need to be urgently addressed. Transformative learning, we saw, is in reality two sides of the same fabric: the students on the one side, the teacher on the other. Transformation had to take place for both and in both, with instructors understanding the necessity for creating new roles for themselves; roles that include being a learning coach, learning facilitator, designer of learning environments, curator, and challenger. Transformation also meant instructors inviting students to take ownership of their learning, with both venturing into a totally new relationship in the classroom, in a dance of coresponsibility. It meant, furthermore, teachers letting go of power and—paradoxically—gaining immense respect and authority as they did so.

In turn, transformation for students meant stepping into self-directed learning, as they empowered themselves to seek information. It also meant they needed to pause and discover themselves anew in the journey; reflecting on the value system lying behind events that occur and behind their own patterns of behavior and habits, as they explored not only the why and the "what-for" of theories, but also the purpose of their own professions. It meant students asking questions—and then being asked to answer them too. They are finding inspiration in the change makers who are championing a major, multidimensional shift in the world. And it meant, too, students accepting the need to take on actions in order to make their learning real—initiatives making a difference in the community and the world.

We saw the wide spread of initiatives that are emerging in different parts of the world, led by pioneering instructors curious to experiment with new approaches to enhance learning. Some arrived at the point of change out of frustration at not being able to capture the interest of their young audience, and others out of the desire to have a more gratifying interaction with their students. Some because they recall how much they suffered themselves, and realize that they don't have to perpetuate a model of teaching that is definitely outdated. And others are motivated because they feel the urgency to fix what has gone seriously wrong in our way of doing business, of handling natural resources, of caring for each other, of finding happiness and fulfillment. Interestingly, in a world that became smaller, the disconnection between what we do today and the impact we are creating, is vanishing. And so is the disconnection between us and nature, between us and others across the globe, between us and the next generations. The power pyramid that thrived on disconnection and abuse of power is crumbling and a new networked world is emerging. We educators have the option to follow to where the younger generation is pointing, or to stand our ground and to be dragged in the direction that the flow is taking us. And while they are impatient, distracted, even confused, they are also seeking meaning, they earnestly want to make a difference, to participate, and not to just be observers and bystanders. As a student said with a sheepish smile to a board room filled with baby boomers, "Excuse me, this is *our* world."

The students of the world can become the actors who, while tackling some of the real challenges of our planet, develop the skills they need. We—and they—don't have to wait for graduation. Management education institutions can become the link connecting the minds and passion of students with the challenges of the community, of policy makers, or of businesses that want to think out of the box. Business schools can become incubators of social entrepreneurs,[1] role models of a new economic system where business becomes again, as in its origin, the vehicle for creating wealth at the service of a real community need.

Dean Katrin Muff of Lausanne Business Schools asked 300 deans and academics in a room: "Close your eyes and envision the world you want to live in." This is what I see: Community, government, policy makers, business schools, faculty, and students merging in new networks, in deeper dialogues, in learning and serving each other. I see economic and social models getting in sync with each other and with the environment, not as an option, but out of necessity. I see extreme polarization painfully evolving into mutual growth. I see a growing understanding of interconnectedness taught to us by Nature; a sense of coresponsibility, with young people around the world stepping into action, and social entrepreneurs inventing solutions that not only don't harm any of the many stakeholders, but do good. I see us noticing that we are at the edge of a cliff, and thoroughly scared of it. But at the same time I see us gaining heightened awareness and consciousness, and a profound awakening of the soul.

The Zeitgeist is out of the bottle. And this is good.

Appendix

The principles we have explored in this book can be applied to a variety of settings, and the readers will probably have recognized many teaching techniques they are currently using, that fall under one or the other principle. As we can see from the large body of scholarly literature referring to each principle, these are not new concepts. Described in one way or another, the principles represent the core of what can make for powerful learning.

Each principle serves as a thinking guide pointing our attention in one direction, and helping us reflect if we are or could be including that aspect into our class. Personal experience and creativity will do the rest, as we find and try out new ways to achieve our goals as educators. In addition, the particular learning outcomes in each discipline and subject set certain boundaries and conditions, to which we need to adjust. Boundaries also provide opportunities to be creative, to challenge and innovate.

What steps can we take to invent our own new ways of enhancing the learning experience?

In the following, you will find a list of questions that can provide guidance and inspiration to adapt and adopt into your particular teaching context.

Checklist for Using the Principles

Overall: Are participants made aware of the importance, impact, and applicability of the learning principles implemented?

Principle: Relevance

Learning is optimal when the focus of the learning is owned by, important and timely for the individual.[1]

Creating Ownership of the Learning

- Have the participants been sufficiently involved in the codesign of the class or course?
- Have the participants created their own personal learning goals and identified milestones to measure their progress?
- Have the criteria of success been defined clearly and jointly with the participants? Have the criteria been defined first by the participants before the instructor provided input and guidance?
- Are the participants free to participate? In what?
- Does the design accommodate each participant's personal learning goals?
- Might any of my activities or attitudes contradict the value given to ownership of the learning? How can I identify, and deal with, or prevent them?
- Do I periodically revisit the design to ensure that it is still relevant for each session?

Just-in-Time Interventions

- As an instructor, am I prepared, do I have the resources I may need?
- Am I prepared to introduce tools and concepts, and do I have the time to use appropriate teaching material when it is most relevant and facilitative of the further learning?
- How do I determine the right timing?
- Am I offering the just-in-time (JIT) interventions as an option, and am I letting the participants decide if the interventions are appropriate?
- Can I ensure that the use of teaching material is genuinely appropriate to the needs of the group and is not just meeting my own needs as an expert to demonstrate my expertise?
- Do I have a sufficiently good grasp of a wide-enough range of material that I can use immediately without much preparation in working "live" with a group?

- Am I making good use of the Matrix of Knowing and Not Knowing, to select the most appropriate processes for Quadrants 1 and 4? (see page 92)

Quadrant 1: Participants realize that they don't know much about a topic, are curious about it, or unsure of their understanding. The learning facilitator can explore what questions the participants have about a theme, to promote ownership of the learning and to make the experience relevant, following the interests in the room.

Quadrant 4: The participants don't know what they don't know. This may be the most frequent assumption of instructors, and it is worth taking a moment to confirm that this is the case. Once it is clear that the participants do not know about a topic, the learning facilitator can wear his "instructor hat" and present the new contents. This role is most powerful when the contents are introduced following a hint—for example, it may be important information for a given project the participants are working on, or for a discussion that is underway. In other words, when it is "just-in-time" as opposed to "just-in-case."

Linking

- Am I connecting each concept with the context of the audience to enable further generalization and application?
- Are there other contexts and conceptual frameworks that need to be connected to the different activities of the program or session?
- What questions can I ask to connect what we just discussed with their own life, present, past, or future?

Balancing Task and Learning

- Does the course as a whole, and its separate components, provide an appropriate balance between a focus on task achievement and a focus on process, what are we learning, and how are we learning it?

- Is there enough time budgeted for debriefs and learning sessions?
- Do we hold a debrief after each session?
- How can we alternate the learning at the personal, professional, team, or organizational level in order to make space for all of them throughout the course?
- Have we made it explicit that we give equal importance to learning contents or concepts and to learning about self or even about the process of learning?

Principle: Tacit Knowledge

Knowledge exists within individuals in implicit forms of which the individual is unaware: It is under-or not fully utilized and can be accessed through guided introspection.

Using Guided Reflection

- Are there sufficient opportunities built into the program to allow dedicated time for reflection on the activities undertaken?
- How can we ensure that participants get personal silent reflection time, in or outside the classroom?
- How do we include writing as a way to create a linear presentation of thoughts?
- What are some activities that can make the guided reflection fun, exciting, interesting?
- Does the design allow the opportunity to ask well-thoughtout, stimulating questions that can help to challenge the habitual frames of reference of the participants?
- What are some "good" questions that can be used?

Using Questions

- What are the best moments to ask the students for their questions?

- How can I design a class or a segment where I can flexibly follow their questions as opposed to deliver what I had in mind?
- What personal obstacles, habits, and personal preferences do I need to overcome to base my interventions on the students' questions?
- What assumptions do I hold about students and their questions?
- What are some creative ideas I can employ when the students are silent, have no questions, and put all the ownership of the learning on me?
- What would qualify as "good questions"?

Principle: Reflection

Reflection is the process of being able to thoughtfully ponder an experience, which can enable greater meaning and learning to be derived from a given situation.

Guided reflection

In addition to the previous questions (see Tacit Knowledge) consider the following:

- How can I bring awareness to the importance of reflection in our life and to how it is related to the topic of my course?
- What rituals of reflection can be brought into the course?
- What are questions the students have themselves, to guide a collective reflection exercise (also their personal reflection exercise)?
- What is the overarching and specific purpose of each activity where I'm guiding their reflection in a certain direction?

Feedback

- What opportunities for feedback can I create so that students develop their habit of reflecting?

- How can I design feedback moments (individual, in pairs, collectively) so that students benefit from reflecting on what happened?

Principle: Self-Awareness

Building self-awareness in people through helping them understand the relation between what they feel, think, and act, and their impact on others, is a crucial step toward their greater personal and professional competence.

Learning and Personality Styles

- Am I using a full range of learning activities that will appeal to the complete range of different learning and personality styles?
- Am I making a conscious check to ensure that the learning and personality styles addressed through different learning activities do not overly reflect my preferences as instructor?
- Have I planned spaces for the group to reflect on how the preferences of others may be influencing their behaviors that we perceive as "strange"?
- Have I included enough activities to help participants learn, explore, discover, and articulate their own learning and personality styles or preferences?
- What is my own learning preference? What is my personality style and how is it expressed in my performance with the students?
- What are my "shadow side" aspects that I should be aware of?

Coaching 1:1

- Does the design offer opportunities to give participants 1:1 coaching support?
- Is there a more formal process of contracting that I can use so participants can be given 1:1 coaching support?

- Am I ensuring to make at least one meaningful contact with each participant?
- Is this individual support helping the participants to increase their self-awareness?
- Have I planned activities to help participants reflect on the impact of their own behavioral patterns?

Principle: Social Learning

Learning emerges through social interaction and, therefore, individuals multiply their learning opportunities.

Exchange of Learnings

- During the class, do I explicitly give time to participants to share their individual learnings?
- What opportunities do I provide for new learning, insights, and frames of reference to emerge spontaneously from the interaction of the participants?
- Are participants made aware of the power of exchanging learnings?
- How are the exchanges captured?

Principle: Paradigm Shift

The most significant learning occurs when individuals are able to shift the perspective by which they habitually view the world, leading to greater understanding, both of their world and of others.

Unfamiliar Environments

- Are there sufficient opportunities for risk-taking and challenge?
- Does the course expose participants to unfamiliar environments and activities that help to surface and challenge their default mental models?

- Is there enough time planned to reflect on, analyze, and debrief the impact of encountering unfamiliar environments, to explore one's deepest assumptions, values, interpretation patterns, and feelings that are triggered?
- Are there opportunities to uncover the participants' underlying assumptions?

Principle: Systems Thinking

We live in a complex, interconnected, cocreated world, and, in order to better understand and tackle individual and organizational issues, we have to take into account the different systems and contexts that mutually influence one another.

Interconnectedness

- How is the systems perspective introduced, presented?
- Does the design include the appropriate focus on the different subsystems, that is, individual, team, organizational, community, environmental, global?
- Are the participants aware of this?

Principle: Integration

People are a combination of mind, body, soul, and emotions, and respond best when all aspects of their being are considered, engaged, and valued.

Appreciative Approach

- Do the type of questions asked, and the overall design of the course, help build an appreciative approach of individual and team strengths?
- Do I feel comfortable being appreciative? How do I show it?
- Are participants' positive qualities, talents, and skills sufficiently recognized, valued, and celebrated?
- What activities will help us in being more appreciative?
- How is success acknowledged?

Safe Environments

- Does the overall environment in all its aspects, both physical and emotional, provide sufficient safety to, and inspire the trust of, participants?
- Do I give time, and use the appropriate tools, to explicitly build a working atmosphere of trust, openness, collaboration, and mutual respect?

Holistic Involvement of the Individual

- Do the different activities and tools used enable participants to engage and express themselves at an emotional and imaginative, as well as an intellectual, level?
- Is the whole mind–body system involved in the learning experience?
- Does the design include sharing the different aspects of the participants' life (family, hobbies, interests, life experiences, etc.)?

Principle: Repetition and Reinforcement

Practice brings mastery and positive reinforcement increases the assimilation.

Sequenced Learning

- Do the different parts of the class or course fit well together into a coherent, logical persuasive whole?
- Does the design provide time for participants to try out new behaviors or skills, and how can I support them as they reflect on their experience, and how address difficulties and obstacles?
- Does the class make good use of summarizing to reinforce learning?
- How are small change attempts identified, supported, reinforced, and celebrated?

Feedback

- Have we clearly defined the criteria to measure success?
- Is periodical feedback included to assess the impact, efficacy, and appropriateness of the design, contents, and interventions of the learning facilitator?
- Do I revisit what I do, based on the feedback I receive?
- Are there measurable ways to assess the results of the different learning outcomes?
- Have I included my peers and the students in answering this question?
- Am I connecting regularly with the participants to support them and provide them feedback to help them reach their goals?

Principle: Learning Facilitator

A specific role exists for an expert in methods and techniques for teaching and learning who can optimize the learning of both individuals and groups.

Learning Coach

- Am I using the full range of learning coach roles (reflector, JIT teacher, coach, facilitator, designer) in the course?
- Am I equally comfortable with all these roles?
- Am I comfortable redesigning "on the go"?
- What can I do to get more comfortable?
- Is the role of the learning coach clear to participants?
- Do I see a gradual transfer of these roles from instructor to the group, going from high intervention to minimal and low?
- Is feedback included to periodically assess the performance and efficacy of the learning facilitator?

Notes

Introduction

1. McCarthy and McCarthy (2006).
2. Kolb and Kolb (2005).
3. Pfeffer and Fong (2002, 2009).
4. Ehrenfeld and Hoffman (2013).

Chapter 1

1. Kimberly and Bouchikhi (2016).
2. Khurana (2010).
3. Hacker and Dreifus (2010).

Chapter 3

1. Rasche and Escudero (2009).
2. http://www.un.org/sustainabledevelopment/sustainable-develop-ment-goals/
3. Kreb (2008).
4. Rimanoczy (2010).
5. Lissack (1999).
6. Ketola (2008).
7. Rimanoczy (2014).
8. Neal (2008).
9. Hörisch, Freeman, and Schaltegger (2014).
10. Scharmer and Kaufer (2013).
11. Gardiner (2014).
12. Mitchell (2012).
13. Rimanoczy (2013).
14. Hoover et al. (2010).
15. Friga, Bettis, and Sullivan (2003).

Chapter 4

1. Rohlin (2012).
2. Rohlin (1984).
3. Rohlin (2007).
4. Rimanoczy and Turner (2008).
5. Rohlin (2002).
6. Rimanoczy (2005).
7. McDonald (2013); Rimanoczy (2010); Schein (2015).
8. Roberts, Rimanoczy, and Drizin (2007).

Chapter 5

1. McCarthy and McCarthy (2006).
2. Kolb and Kolb (2005).

Chapter 6

1. My gratitude to Boris Drizin and Paul Roberts, who joined me and engaged many hours of passionate reflection, research, and discussions to develop the coding and conceptual framework of the ten principles. Roberts, Rimanoczy, and Drizin (2007).
2. Vail (1996).
3. Freire (1970).
4. Eisler (2000).
5. Eisler (1994).
6. Weisman (2008).
7. Norberg-Hodge (2000).
8. Several conceptual frameworks of human development have studied the evolution of human consciousness and classified it into levels or stages, from "me" (egocentric) to "us" (ethnocentric) to "all of us" (world-centric). See: Integral Theory: Wilber (2001); Spiral Dynamics: Beck and Cowan (2014); Orders of Consciousness: Kegan (1994); Moral Development: Fowler and Levin (1984).
9. Knowles (1970).
10. Raelin (2000).

11. Dewey (1938).
12. Lindeman (1926).
13. Kolb (1984).
14. Vygotsky (1962, 1978); Lave (1988). Lave formulates it as a principle herself: "Knowledge needs to be presented in an authentic context, that is, settings and applications that would normally involve that knowledge." Also Lave and Wenger (1991).
15. Lewin (1951).
16. De Jong (2006).
17. Cunningham (1981).
18. Revans (1982).

Chapter 7

1. Polanyi (1958).
2. Nonaka (1991).
3. Wenger (1998).
4. Freire (1970).
5. Eisler (1988).
6. McDonald (2013).

Chapter 8

1. Dewey (1916, 1938).
2. Kolb (1984).
3. Lewin (1951).
4. Argyris (1982).
5. Kegan and Lahey (2001).
6. Brookfield (1995); Mezirow (2000).
7. Brookfield (1988).
8. Mezirow (1990).

Chapter 9

1. See *Encyclopedia* of Philosophy, 1967.
2. James (1890).

3. Freud (1900).

4. Kegan (1994).

5. Torbert (1991).

6. Wilber (2001).

7. Rogers (1961).

8. Jung (1924).

9. Myers-Briggs (1962).

10. Senge (1990).

11. Goleman (1996).

12. Rimanoczy (2010, 2013).

13. Mezirow (1990, 1991).

14. Freire (1970).

15. Argyris (1982).

16. Schön (1983).

17. Brookfield (1998).

18. Cranton (1994).

19. Kegan and Lahey (2001).

20. Siebenhüner (2000).

21. Wilber (2004).

22. Honey and Mumford (2006).

Chapter 10

1. Vygotsky (1968, 1978).

2. Lave and Wenger (1991).

3. Wenger (1998).

4. Bandura (1977).

Chapter 11

1. Kuhn (1970).

2. Kegan (1994).

3. Torbert (1991).

4. Wilber (2001).

5. Kendig (1990).

6. Cranton (1994).

7. Mezirow (1991).

8. Brookfield (1995).

9. Argyris (1982).

10. Schön (1983).

11. Senge (1990).

12. Freire (1970).

13. Horton et al. (1990).

14. Belenky et al. (1986).

15. Gilligan (1982).

16. Mezirow (1991).

Chapter 12

1. von Bertalanffy (1968).

2. Capra (1996, 2004).

3. Wiener (1948).

4. Ashby (1956).

5. Schultz (1993).

6. Dilts et al. (1980).

7. Jackson (1991).

8. Rivlin (2015).

9. Senge (1990); Sterman (2000).

10. Hodgson (2001).

11. Capra (1996, 2004).

12. Kegan (1994); Torbert (1991); Wilber (2001).

13. Elkington (1998); Hawken (1993); Hawken, Lovins, and Lovins (2013).

14. Rimanoczy (2016).

15. Köhler (1970, 1929).

16. Wertheimer (1938).

17. Koffka (2001).

18. Lewin (1951).

Chapter 13

1. Goleman (1996).

2. Tisdell (2001).

Chapter 14

1. Watson (1970).
2. Skinner (1971, 1974).
3. Thorndike (1932).
4. Maslow (1943).
5. Ausubel (1968).
6. Bandura (1997).
7. Dewey (1938).
8. Rogers (1961).
9. Cooperrider and Whitney (1999).
10. Social Constructionism is a sociological theory of knowledge, which looks into the way individuals and groups participate in the creation of their perceived reality. The concept was introduced in the United States in 1967 by Berger and Luckmann, in their book *The Social Construction of Reality.*

Chapter 15

1. Piaget (1952, 1972).
2. Rogers (1961).
3. Knowles (1970).
4. Freire (1970).
5. Horton et al. (1990).
6. Candy and Brookfield (1991).
7. Kolb (1984).
8. Mezirow (2000).
9. Schön (1983).
10. Cranton (1994).
11. Walsh (2011).
12. Thomas, Thomas, and Wilson (2013).

Chapter 16

1. Barr and Tagg (1995).
2. Carey (2015).

3. See Appendix for a Guide of Question to design.

4. Finkel (1999).

5. Savery (2015).

6. Savin-Baden (2000).

Chapter 17

1. Scharmer and Kaufer (2013).

2. Bergmann and Sams (2012).

3. McGregor (2011).

Chapter 18

1. Doran (1981).

2. Milton, Pollio, and Eison (1986).

3. Strong, Davis, and Hawks (2004).

4. Sadler and Good (2006). See also Vander Schee (2011).

5. Boud and Falchikov (2007); Nicol and MacFarlane-Dick (2006); Crisp (2010); McCarthy (2013).

6. Cassidy (2007); Kirby and Downs (2007); Thompson, Pilgrim, and Oliver (2005).

7. Evans, McKenna, and Oliver (2005).

8. Leach (2000).

9. Thompson, Pilgrim, and Oliver (2005).

10. Cherepinsky (2011).

11. Becker, Geer, and Hughes (1968).

Chapter 19

1. Clarke, Dameron, and Durand (2013).

Chapter 20

1. Wood (2014).

2. ARTEM, www.mines-nancy.univ-lorraine.fr/content/ artem-art-technologie-management

3. Ulrike et al. (2014).

4. In one two-year longitudinal study, undergraduate students at MUM increased significantly on Cattell's Culture Fair Intelligence Test and Hick's reaction time, compared to a control group. A bibliography of peer-reviewed research on the effects of Transcendental Meditation on improved intelligence, creativity, and learning ability, as well as other findings, can be found at www.tm.org/research-on-meditation

5. Muff et al. (2013).

Chapter 21

1. Starkey and Hatchuel (2014); Readings (1997).

Appendix

1. Roberts, Rimanoczy, and Drizin (2007).

References

Argyris, C. 1982. *Reasoning, Learning and Action: Individual and Organizational*. San Francisco: Jossey Bass.

Ashby, W.R. 1956. *An Introduction to Cybernetics*. London: Chapman & Hail.

Ausubel, D.P. 1968. *Educational Psychology: A Cognitive View*. New York: Holt, Rinehart & Winston.

Bandura, A. 1977. *Social/Earning Theory*. New York: General Learning.

Barr, R., and J. Tagg. 1995. "From Teaching to Learning: A New Paradigm for Undergraduate Education." *Change* 27, no. 6, pp. 12–25.

Beck, D.E., and C. Cowan. 2014. *Spiral Dynamics: Mastering Values, Leadership and Change*. New York: John Wiley & Sons.

Becker, H.S., B. Geer, and E. Hughes. 1968. *Making the Grade*. New York: John Wiley and Sons.

Belenky, M., B.M. Clinchy, N.R. Goldberger, and J. Tarule. 1986. *Women's Ways of Knowing: The Development of Self, Mind, and Voice*. New York: Basic Books.

Berger, P.L., and T. Luckmann. 1967. *The Social Construction of Reality*. London: Penguin Press.

Bergmann, J., and A. Sams. 2012. *Flip Your Classroom: Reach Every Student in Every Class Every Day*. ISTE-ASCD.

Boud, D., and N. Falchikov, eds. 2007. *Rethinking Assessment for Higher Education: Learning for the Longer Term*. London: Routledge.

Brookfield, S. 1988. "Developing Critically Reflective Practitioners: A Rationale for Training Educators of Adults." *Training Educators of Adults: The Theory and Practice of Graduate Adult Education*, pp. 317–38.

Brookfield, S. 1998. "Critically Reflective Practice." *Journal of Continuing Education in the Health Professions* 18, no. 4, pp. 197–205.

Brookfield, S.D. 1995. *Becoming a Critically Reflective Teacher*. San Francisco: Jossey-Bass.

Candy, P.C., and S. Brookfield. 1991. *Self-Direction for Lifelong Learning. A Comprehensive Guide to Theory and Practice*. San Francisco: Jossey-Bass.

Capra, F. 1996. *The Web of Life*. London: Harper Collins.

Capra, F. 2004. *The Hidden Connections: A Science For Sustainable Living*. New York: Anchor Books.

Carey, K. 2015. *The End of College: Creating the Future of Learning and the University of Everywhere*. New York: Penguin Books.

Cassidy, S. 2007. "Assessing 'Inexperienced' Students' Ability to Self-assess: Exploring Links with Learning Style and Academic Personal Control." *Assessment & Evaluation in Higher Education* 32, no. 3, pp. 313–30.

Cherepinsky, V. 2011. "Self-Reflective Grading: Getting Students to Learn from Their Mistakes." *PRIMUS* 21, no. 3, pp. 294–301. Retrieved from http://search.proquest.com.ezproxylocal.library.nova.edu/docview/864940762?accountid=6579

Clarke, T., S. Dameron, and T. Durand. 2013. "Strategies for Business Schools in a Multi-Polar World." *Education + Training* 55, pp. 323–35.

Cooperrider, D.L., and D. Whitney. 1999. *Collaborating for Change: Appreciative Inquiry.* San Francisco, CA: Barrett-Koehler Communication.

Cranton, P. 1994. *Understanding and Promoting Transformative Learning: A Guide for Educators of Adults. Jossey-Bass Higher and Adult Education Series.* San Francisco: Jossey-Bass.

Crisp, G.T. 2012. "Integrative Assessment: Reframing Assessment Practice for Current and Future Learning." *Assessment & Evaluation in Higher Education*, iFirst Article.

Cunningham, I. 1981. "Self Managed Learning and Independent Study." In *Management Self-Development: Concepts and Practices*, eds. T. Boydell and M. Pedler. Hants: Gower.

De Jong, T. 2006. *Technological Advances in Inquiry Learning.* New York: Science.

Dewey, J. 1916. *Democracy and Education: An Introduction to the Philosophy of Education.* New York: Free Press.

Dewey, J. 1938. *Experience and Education.* New York: Collier Books.

Dilts, R., J. Grinder, J. Delozier, and R. Bandler. 1980. *Neuro-Linguistic Programming: Volume I: The Study of the Structure of Subjective Experience*, 2. Cupertino, CA: Meta Publications.

Doran, G.T. 1981. "There's a S.M.A.R.T. Way to Write Management's Goals and Objectives." *Management Review (AMA FORUM)* 70, no. 11, pp. 35–36.

Ehrenfeld, J., and A. Hoffman. 2013. *Flourishing: A Frank Conversation about Sustainability.* Redwood City, CA: Stanford University Press.

Eisler, R.T. 1988. *The Chalice and the Blade: Our History, Our Future.* New York: Harper & Row.

Eisler, R.T. 1994. From Domination to Partnership: The Hidden Subtext for Sustainable Change. *Journal of Organizational Change Management* 7, no. 4, pp. 32–46.

Eisler, R.T. 2000. *Tomorrow's Children: A Blueprint for Partnership Education in the 21st Century.* Boulder, CO: Westview Press.

Elkington, J. 1998. *Cannibals with Forks: The Triple Bottom Line of 21st Century Business.* Gabriola Island, BC, Canada: New Society Publishers.

Evans, A., C. McKenna, and M. Oliver. 2005. "Trainees' Perspectives on the Assessment and Self-assesment of Surgical Skills." *Assessment & Evaluation in Higher Education* 30, no. 2, pp. 163–74.

Finkel, D.L. 1999. *Teaching with Your Mouth Shut.* Portsmouth, NH: Boynton/Cook Publishers.

Fowler, J.W., and R.W. Levin. 1984. *Stages of Faith: The Psychology of Human Development and the Quest for Meaning.* San Francisco, CA: Harper & Row.

Freire, P. 1970. *Pedagogy of the Oppressed.* New York: Seabury.

Freud, S. 1900. *The Interpretation of Dreams.* SE, 4–5.

Friga, P.N., R.A. Bettis, and R.S. Sullivan. 2003. "Changes in Graduate Management Education and New Business School Strategies for the 21st Century." *Academy of Management Learning & Education* 2, pp. 233–49.

Gardiner, B. 2012. "Business Skills and Buddhist Mindfulness." *The Wall Street Journal.* Retrieved from www.wsj.com/articles/SB10001424052702303816504577305820565167202

Gilligan, C. 1982. *In a Different Voice.* Cambridge: Harvard University Press.

Goleman, D. 1996. *Emotional Intelligence.* London: Bloomsbury Publishing.

Hacker, A., and C. Dreifus. 2010. *Higher Education? How Colleges Are Wasting Our Money and Failing Our Kids and What We Can Do About It.* New York: St. Martin's Griffin.

Hawken, P. 1993. *The Ecology of Commerce.* New York: Harper Collins.

Hawken, P., A.B. Lovins, and L.H. Lovins. 2013. *Natural Capitalism: The Next Industrial Revolution.* New York: Routledge.

Hodgson, B. 2001. *Economics as Moral Science.* New York: Springer Science & Business Media.

Honey, P., and A. Mumford. 2006. *The Learning Styles Questionnaire: 80-Item Version.* Maidenhead, Berkshire, UK: Peter Honey Publications Limited.

Hoover, J.D., R.C. Giambatista, R.L. Sorenson, and W.H. Bommer. 2010. Assessing the Effectiveness of Whole Person Learning Pedagogy in Skill Acquisition. *Academy of Management Learning & Education* 9, no. 2, pp. 192–203.

Hörisch, J., R.E. Freeman, and S. Schaltegger. 2014. "Applying Stakeholder Theory in Sustainability Management Links, Similarities, Dissimilarities, and a Conceptual Framework." *Organization & Environment* 27, no. 4, pp. 328–46.

Horton, M., P. Freire, B. Bell, and J. Gaventa. 1990. *We Make the Road by Walking: Conversations on Education and Social Change.* Philadelphia: Temple University Press.

Jackson, M.C. 1991. *Systems Methodology for the Management Sciences.* New York: Plenum Press.

James, W. (1890) 1950. *The Principles of Psychology.*

Jung, C.G. May 1924. *Analytical Psychology and Education.*

Kegan, R. 1994. *In Over Our Heads: The Mental Demands of Modern Life.* Cambridge, MA: Harvard University Press.

Kegan, R., and L.L. Lahey. 2001. *How the Way We Talk Can Change the Way We Work: Seven Languages for Transformation.* San Francisco: Jossey-Bass.

Kendig, M., ed. 1990. *Alfred Korzybski: Collected Writings, 1920–1950*. Institute of General Semantics.

Ketola, T. 2008. "A Holistic Corporate Responsibility Model: Integrating Values, Discourses and Actions." *Journal of Business Ethics* 80, no. 3, pp. 419–35.

Khurana, R. 2010. *From Higher Aims to Hired Hands: The Social Transformation of American Business Schools and the Unfulfilled Promise of Management as a Profession*. Princeton, NJ: Princeton University Press.

Kimberly, J.R., and H. Bouchikhi. 2016. "Disruption on Steroids: Sea Change in the Worlds of Higher Education in General and Business Education in Particular." *Journal of Leadership & Organizational Studies* 23, no. 1, pp. 5–12.

Kirby, N., and C. Downs. 2007. "Self-Assessment and the Disadvantaged Student: Potential for Encouraging Self-Regulated Learning?" *Assessment & Evaluation in Higher Education* 32, no. 4, pp. 475–94.

Knowles, M. 1970. *The Modern Practice of Adult Education: Andragogy Versus Pedagogy*. New York: Association Press.

Koffka, K. 2001. *Principles of Gestalt psychology*. London: Routledge.

Köhler, W. (1929) 1970. *Gestalt Psychology: An Introduction to New Concepts in Modern Psychology*. New York: WW Norton & Company.

Kolb, D. 1984. *Experiential Learning: Experience as the Source of Learning and Development*. Englewood Cliffs, NJ: Prentice Hall.

Kolb, A.Y., and D.A. Kolb. 2005. "Learning Styles and Learning Spaces: Enhancing Experiential Learning in Higher Education." *Academy of Management Learning & Education* 4, no. 2, pp. 193–212.

Kreb, C.J. 2008. *The Ecological World View*. Oakland, CA: University of California Press.

Kuhn, T.S. 1970. *The Structure of Scientific Revolutions*. 2nd ed. Chicago: University of Chicago Press.

Lave, J. 1988. *Cognition in Practice: Mind, Mathematics, and Culture in Everyday Life*. Cambridge, MA: Cambridge University Press.

Lave, J., and E. Wenger. 1991. *Situated Learning: Legitimate Peripheral Participation*. Cambridge, MA: Cambridge University Press.

Leach, L. 2000. *Self Directed Learning: Theory and Practice*. Sydney: University of Technology [Unpublished PhD thesis].

Lewin, K. 1951. *Field Theory in Social Science: Selected Theoretical Papers*, ed. C. Dorwin. New York: Harper & Row.

Lindeman, E.C. 1926. *The Meaning of Adult Education*. New York: New Republic.

Lissack, M.R. 1999. "Complexity: The Science, Its Vocabulary, and Its Relation to Organizations." *Emergence* 1, no. 1, pp. 110–26.

Maslow, A.H. 1943. "A Theory of Human Motivation." *Psychological Review* 50, no. 4, p. 370.

McCarthy, B., and D. McCarthy. 2006. *Teaching Around the 4MAT® Cycle: Designing Instruction for Diverse Learners with Diverse Learning Styles.* Thousand Oaks, CA: Corwin Press.

McCarthy, G. 2013. "Authentic Assessment—Key to Learning." In *Innovative Business School Teaching—Engaging the Millennial Generation,* eds. E. Doyle, P. Buckley, and C. Carroll, 81–92. United Kingdom: Routledge.

McDonald, R. 2013. *A Practical Guide to Educating for Responsibility in Management and Business.* New York: Business Expert Press.

McGregor, G. 2011. "Engaging Gen Y in Schooling: The Need for an Egalitarian Ethos of Education." *Pedagogy Culture & Society* 19, no. 1, p. 1. Retrieved from http://search.proquest.com.ezproxylocal.library.nova.edu/docview/870470988?accountid=6579

Mezirow, J. 1990. "How Critical Reflection Triggers Transformative Learning." *Fostering Critical Reflection in Adulthood,* pp. 1–20.

Mezirow, J. 1991. *Transformative Dimensions of Adult Learning.* San Francisco: Jossey-Bass.

Mezirow, J. 2000. *Learning as Transformation: Critical Perspectives on a Theory in Progress. The Jossey-Bass Higher and Adult Education Series.* San Francisco: Jossey-Bass.

Milton, O., H.R. Pollio, and J.A. Eison. 1986. *Making Sense of College Grades.* San Francisco: Jossey-Bass.

Mitchell, S.F. 2012. *An Empirical Investigation: How Small to Mid-sized Enterprises use Innovation on the Path Toward Ecological Sustainability* [Doctoral Dissertation]. University of New Hampshire.

Muff, K., T. Dyllick, M. Drewell, J. North, P. Shrivastava, and J. Haertle. 2013. *Management Education for the World: A Vision for Business Schools Serving People and the Planet.* Cheltenham, UK/Northampton, MA: Edward Elgar Publishing.

Myers-Briggs, I. 1962. *The Myers-Briggs Type Indicator Manual.* Princeton, NJ: Educational Testing Service.

Neal, J.A. 2008. *Leadership and Spirituality in the Workplace.* Retrieved July 15, 2009 from www.judineal.com/pages/pubs/leadership.htm

Nicol, D.J., and D. Macfarlane-Dick. 2006. "Formative Assessment and Self-Regulated Learning: A Model and Seven Principles of Good Feedback Practice." *Studies in Higher Education* 31, no. 2, pp. 199–218.

Nonaka, I. 1991. "The Knowledge-Creating Company." *Harvard Business Review,* pp. 96–104.

Norberg-Hodge, H. 2000. *Ancient Futures: Learning from Ladakh.* London: Random House.

Pfeffer, J., and C.T. Fong. 2002. The End of Business Schools? Less Success than Meets the Eye." *Academy of Management Learning & Education* 1, no. 1, pp. 78–95.

Pfeffer, J., and C.T. Fong. 2009. Renaissance and Renewal in Management Studies: Relevance Regained." *European Management Review* 6, no. 3, pp. 141–48.

Piaget, J. 1952. *The Origins of Intelligence in Children*, 18–1952, Vol. 8, no. 5. New York: International Universities Press.

Piaget, J. 1972. "Intellectual Evolution from Adolescence to Adulthood." *Human Development* 15, no. 1, pp. 1–12.

Polanyi, M. 1958. *Personal Knowledge: Towards a Post-Critical Philosophy*. London: Routledge.

Raelin, J. 2000. *Work-Based Learning: The New Frontier of Management Development*. Upper Saddle River, NJ: Prentice Hall.

Rasche, A., and M. Escudero. 2009. "Leading Change: The Role of the Principles for Responsible Management Education." *Zeitschrift für Wirtschafts-und Unternehmensethik* 10, no. 2, p. 244.

Readings, B. 1997. *The University in Ruins*. Cambridge, MA: Harvard University Press.

Revans, R. 1982. *The Origins and Growth of Action Learning*. London: Chartwell Bratt.

Rimanoczy, I. 2005. *Principios y Elementos de Action Reflection Learning* [dissertation]. Buenos Aires: Universidad de Palermo.

Rimanoczy, I.B. 2010. *Business Leaders Committing to and Fostering Sustainability Initiatives* [doctoral dissertation]. Teachers College, Columbia University.

Rimanoczy, I. 2013. *Big Bang Being: Developing the Sustainability Mindset*. Sheffield: Greenleaf Publishing.

Rimanoczy, I. 2014. "A Matter of Being: Developing Sustainability-Minded Leaders." *Journal of Management for Global Sustainability* 2, no. 1, pp. 95–122.

Rimanoczy, I. June 2016. "A Holistic Learning Approach for Responsible Management Education." In *Educating for Responsible Management: Putting Theory into Practice*, eds. R. Sunley and J. Leigh. Sheffield, UK: Greenleaf Publishing. (Forthcoming).

Rimanoczy, I., and E. Turner. 2008. *Action Reflection Learning: Solving Real Business Problems by Connecting Learning with Earning*. Palo Alto: Davies Black Publishing.

Rivlin, A.M. 2015. *Systematic Thinking for Social Action*. Washington, DC: The Brookings Institution.

Roberts, P., I. Rimanoczy, and B. Drizin. 2007. "Principles and Elements of ARL." MiL Concepts 1.

Rogers, C.R. 1961. *On Becoming a Person: A Therapist's View of Psychology*. Boston: Houghton Mifflin.

Rohlin, L. 1984. "An Action Perspective on Management and Management Development." In *Trends in Management and Management Development*. Lund: MiL Management Mission.

Rohlin, L., ed. 2002. *Earning While Learning in Global Leadership: The Volvo MiL Partnership*. Lund: MiL Publications.

Rohlin, L. 2007. Strategic Leadership: Quest for a New Paradigm. *MiL Concepts* 2/2007.

Rohlin, L. 2012. Action Reflection Learning. *MiL Concepts* 9/2012.

Sadler, P.M., and E. Good. 2006. "The Impact of Self- and Peer-Grading on Student Learning." *Educational Assessment* 11, no. 1, pp. 1–31.

Savery, J.R. 2015. "Overview of Problem-Based Learning: Definitions and Distinctions." *Essential Readings in Problem-Based Learning: Exploring and Extending the Legacy of Howard S. Barrows*, pp. 5–15.

Savin-Baden, M. 2000. *Problem-Based Learning in Higher Education: Untold Stories: Untold Stories*. UK: McGraw-Hill Education.

Scharmer, O., and K. Kaufer. 2013. *Leading from the Emerging future from Ego-System to Eco-System Economies*. San Francisco: Berrett-Koehler Publishers.

Schein, S. 2015. *A New Psychology for Sustainability Leadership*. Sheffield: Greenleaf Publishing.

Schön, D.A. 1983. *The Reflective Practitioner: How Professionals Think in Action*. Vol. 5126. New York: Basic Books.

Schultz, S.J. 1993. *Family Systems Thinking*. Northvale, NJ: Jason Aronson.

Senge, P. 1990. *The Fifth Discipline: The Art and Science of the Learning Organization*. New York: Currency Doubleday.

Siebenhüner, B. 2000. "Homo Sustinens—Towards a New Conception of Humans for the Science of Sustainability." *Ecological Economics* 32, no. 1, pp. 15–25.

Skinner, B.F. 1971. *Beyond Freedom and Dignity*. New York: Knopf.

Skinner, B.F. 1974. *About Behaviorism*. New York: Knopf.

Starkey, K., and A. Hatchuel. 2014. "Back to the Future of Management Research." In *The Institutional Development of Business Schools*, eds. A.M. Pettigrew, E. Cornuel, and U. Hommel, 270–93. New York: Oxford University Press.

Sterman, J.D. 2000. *Business Dynamics: Systems Thinking and Modeling for a Complex World*. Vol. 19. Boston: Irwin/McGraw-Hill.

Strong, B., M. Davis, and V. Hawks. 2004. "Self-Grading in Large General Education Classes: A Case Study." *College Teaching* 52, no. 2, pp. 52–57. Retrieved from http://search.proquest.com.ezproxylocal.library.nova.edu/docview/274595683?accountid=6579

Thomas, H., L. Thomas, and A. Wilson. 2013. *Promises Fulfilled and Unfulfilled in Management Education: Reflections on the Role, Impact and Future of Management Education.* Bingley, England: Emerald Group.

Thompson, G., A. Pilgrim, and K. Oliver. 2005. "Self-Assessment and Reflective Learning for First-year Geography Students: A Simple Guide or Simply Misguided?" *Journal of Geography in Higher Education* 29, no. 3, pp. 403–20.

Thorndike, E. 1932. *The Fundamentals of Learning.* New York: AMS Press Inc.

Tisdell, E.J. 2001. *Spirituality in Adult and Higher Education.* ERIC Digest.

Torbert, W.R. 1991. *The Power of Balance: Transforming Self, Society, and Scientific Inquiry.* Newbery Park: Sage.

Turner, E. 2013. *Gentle Interventions for Team Coaching: Little Things that Make a Big Difference.* Fort Lauderdale, FL: CreateSpace.

Ulrike, G., E. Davis, G. Bowser, J. Jiang, and M. Brown. 2014. "Creating Global Leaders with Sustainability Mindsets." *Journal of Teaching in Travel & Tourism* 14, no. 2, pp. 164–83.

Vail, P. 1996. *Learning as a Way of Being.* San Francisco: Jossey Bass.

Vander Schee, B.A. 2011. "Let Them Decide: Student Performance and Self-Selection of Weights Distribution." *Journal of Education for Business* 86, no. 6, p. 352.

von Bertalanffy, L. 1968. *General Systems Theory.* New York: Braziller.

Vygotsky, L.S. 1968. *Thought and Language.* Cambridge, MA: MIT Press.

Vygotsky, L.S. 1978. *Mind in Society.* Cambridge, MA: Harvard University Press.

Walsh, J. 2011. "Presidential Address: Embracing the Sacred in Our Secular Scholarly World." *Academy of Management Review* 36, pp. 215–34.

Watson, J.B. 1970. *Behaviorism.* New York: The Norton Library.

Weisman, A. 2008. *Gaviotas: A Village to Reinvent the World.* White River Junction, VT: Chelsea Green Publishing.

Wenger, E. 1998. *Communities of Practice: Learning, Meaning and Identity.* Cambridge: Cambridge University Press.

Wertheimer, M. 1938. *Gestalt Theory.* In *A Source Book of Gestalt Psychology*, ed. W.D. Ellis, 1–11. London, England: Routledge & Kegan Paul. (Original work published 1924).

Wiener, N. 1948. *Cybernetics, or Control and Communication in the Animal and the Machine.* Cambridge: MIT Press.

Wilber, K. 2001. *Integral Psychology: Consciousness, Spirit, Psychology, Therapy.* Shambhala Publications.

Wilber, K. 2004. *Introduction to Integral Theory and Practice: IOS Basic and the AQAL Map.*

Wood, G. September 2014. "The Future of College?" *The Atlantic.* Retrieved from www.theatlantic.com/magazine/archive/2014/09/the-future-of-college/375071/

Index